TOUCHED BY DIVINE LOVE

TOUCHED BY DIVINE LOVE

A PERSONAL JOURNEY INTO THE UNKNOWN

SAMANTHA RICHARDS

BALBOA.
PRESS

A DIVISION OF HAY HOUSE

Balboa Press books may be ordered through booksellers or by contacting:

Balboa Press
A Division of Hay House
1663 Liberty Drive
Bloomington, IN 47403
www.balboapress.com.au
1-(877) 407-4847

ISBN: 978-1-4525-1064-4 (sc)
ISBN: 978-1-4525-1067-5 (e)

Because of the dynamic nature of the Internet, any web addresses or links contained in this book may have changed since publication and may no longer be valid. The views expressed in this work are solely those of the author and do not necessarily reflect the views of the publisher, and the publisher hereby disclaims any responsibility for them.

The author of this book does not dispense medical advice or prescribe the use of any technique as a form of treatment for physical, emotional, or medical problems without the advice of a physician, either directly or indirectly. The intent of the author is only to offer information of a general nature to help you in your quest for emotional and spiritual well-being. In the event you use any of the information in this book for yourself, which is your constitutional right, the author and the publisher assume no responsibility for your actions.

Any people depicted in stock imagery provided by Thinkstock are models, and such images are being used for illustrative purposes only.
Certain stock imagery © Thinkstock.

Printed in the United States of America

Balboa Press rev. date: 06/20/2013

CONTENTS

Acknowledgements

The list of people I would like to thank is so long that an entire book would be needed to mention them all. If I have missed anyone, know that I am grateful for the belief you have had in me and in my gifts.

My ever-patient husband, Nick, and children, Joshua and Emily, have loved, encouraged, and supported me on this journey. I thank them for being such amazing people.

Faye Wilson will always have a special place in my heart as the person who nurtured me when I reached rock bottom and didn't think I could get back up again.

Julie Mills recognised something in me that I was unable to see. She offered to help me investigate my strengths and identify what moves my soul. I had never experienced such generosity before. Her kindness humbled me and still does.

Andrew Perry helped me pinpoint my dreams and encouraged me to pursue them. His confidence in me gave me the courage to believe in myself.

Gina Karaolglan read my work and offered insight and advice that made this book come to life. The ongoing support of this wonderful and honest friend has on many occasions proved to me that I am on the right path.

Tony Jenkins is a special man who helped me to overcome my fear of singing and to hear a voice I never knew I had. Now I sing all of the time, and because I can sing, I have overcome my fear of public speaking.

I thank my family and friends for their love and support during my journey and for simply being themselves.

I thank my students, who allow me to continue learning even as I teach them.

To all readers I offer deep, heartfelt thanks for taking the time to explore this book, which I hope will help you on your own great adventure.

Finally, I thank Mother Earth for letting us live on her and providing all the resources we need to survive, and I thank the universal energies of life for giving me the will, strength, and courage to bring my dreams to fruition.

INTRODUCTION

I am excited and honoured to be a part of your journey, and I thank you for allowing me the privilege of sharing the knowledge I have gained whilst travelling my own path.

I do not profess to be an all-knowing guru. My voyage is a work in progress, but during my journey I have been blessed with a greater understanding of myself, including how to face my demons and the fears that have reared their ugly heads. By confronting my fears, I have gained a greater self-awareness, spiritually and personally. I call this my spiritual reality. This truth that lies within me is based solely on the teachings of self.

You and I may travel on parallel paths, yet these paths will be coloured differently. This knowledge is the fruit of spiritual self-realisation, growth, and enlightenment, and reveals the awe-inspiring beauty of our individuality.

What can you expect to achieve by reading this book? First and foremost, I hope you will gain a greater self-awareness both spiritually and personally, which will allow you to understand more profoundly the things that you do and why and how you do them. Once you reach this level of understanding, you will discover opportunities that you may not previously have realised, and your deeper awareness of self will position you to take advantage of them.

I have often been asked, "How can I get a hotline to God?" The only answer that I can reasonably give is that the speed at which you develop is entirely up to you. It is determined by the amount of time you invest in doing the required work.

The word *psychic* is derived from the Greek word *psychikos*, which means "of the mind" or "mental" and refers, in part, to the human mind. The Greek word *psyche* means "soul" or "spirit." Therefore I translate the word *psychic* as "mind of the soul" or "mind of the spirit."

This book details how I gained self-awareness in all facets of my life. I will share the processes that I went through, some exhilarating and others downright frustrating. I hope to aid in your personal and spiritual growth, helping you to develop your psychic abilities.

Once again, thank you for allowing me to be a part of your journey. I am thrilled to be walking beside you during your great odyssey of self-discovery.

Journey into the Unknown

This journey has not always been one that I cared to make. Raised a Catholic, I was taught to believe in certain things and in particular ways. Although I was never good at being told what to do or what to believe, I followed my religion.

As I grew, I found myself questioning what I was being taught. I became a thorn in the side of all authority figures who couldn't give me reasonable answers to my queries. "Because the Bible says so," or "This is the Word of the Lord," and (my favourite) "Because it has always been that way" were never responses that I could accept.

I began to play up at school and was asked to leave by at least two schools, one of which my niece ended up attending. She told me that some of the nuns remembered me. I was asked to leave that school when I was nine. What a legacy! I was the classic case of a child needing to be understood.

—ooOoo—

As a child, I could communicate with the spirits of the dead. I saw winged creatures, which I believed to be angels, and would hear them as clearly as if I were having a conversation with a living person. I was often called odd by people who would hear me having conversations with beings they could not see. The spirits would have me stop people on the street and relay messages, which would make the recipients feel uncomfortable. Having a thirteen-year-old girl tell them things she couldn't possibly know was very disconcerting.

I realised after a while that what was normal for me was not normal for society, so I tried to conform. Over time, I learned to ignore the entities that wanted messages sent. Eventually, they stopped showing themselves to me, but I would always get verbal requests. I never complied—until my first date with a boy.

I was an athlete and had little interest in boys until I was about sixteen years old. My physical training and dysfunctional schooling took up most of my time until I was around eighteen. I met a young man in a pub who invited me out to dinner. He was blonde and cute, so I agreed.

We went to a restaurant in London and ordered our meals. Unfortunately, I felt the familiar sensation of a spirit entity beginning to make its presence known. My head seemed to be inside a clamp, and there was a buzzing in my right ear. I knew the spirit was about to speak. Silently, I told it to go away. It didn't, and I began squirming uncomfortably in my seat. My date asked me if I was all right.

As he posed the question, a little girl about four to six years old materialised beside him. She was pretty, wore a little white dress, and had beautiful blonde hair and blue eyes. She was rosy cheeked and had a huge grin plastered all over her little face. She told me she was my date's sister.

Selfishly, I didn't want to ruin my evening, but the little girl pleaded with me to pass a message on to her brother. How could I refuse her?

I looked at my date and blurted out that his sister was standing beside him. I gave him a description of her, explaining that she wanted him to know that she was happy and that it wasn't his fault that she had died. He was to stop feeling guilty.

He went as white as a sheet and asked me to repeat what I had said, so I did. He began to cry and through his tears told me that his little sister had drowned when she was four, a year younger than he was at the time. She had fallen into water, and since he couldn't swim, he was unable to help her. He had lived with the guilt ever since, believing that her death was his fault.

Suddenly, he focussed on me with quiet fury. He stood up and told me that I was a freak and that he never wanted to see me again.

I was shattered, since I didn't understand that what I had done was wrong. Of course, I now realise the enormity of what happened, including the pain he was carrying, but back then I had no idea. In my head, I agreed with him and began reiterating to myself that I was a freak.

Unfortunately, the incidents kept occurring and I got little reprieve from the onslaught even when I reached adulthood.

When I was nineteen, my girlfriend Katherine and I visited my sister Nicky in Somerset, UK. She and her husband were living in an old manor house owned by his parents. Kath and I were shown to our room. There was nothing out of the ordinary about it. Kath entered first. As I stepped over the threshold, I felt an awful chill run through my body. The room went freezing and I could see my breath. "Get out!" a malevolent voice hissed at me. I grabbed Kath's hand and ran from the room. She told me that she had also felt the room go cold.

We spent the evening laughing and eating with my family. (I didn't drink alcohol back then, and even today I may have only a glass or two a week.) We decided that nothing had happened, that we were just spooked because the house was so old.

At about midnight, we wearily made our way to bed. The temperature in the room was normal as we entered. Nothing was amiss when we climbed into our beds and started chatting.

Out of nowhere, I felt a presence close to my face. It breathed cold air onto me and shouted, "I told you to get out. Go now!" I screamed, jumped out of bed, and asked Kath if I could climb into bed with her. In my naiveté, I thought the entity would leave us alone if we shared a bed. Safety in numbers. We hid under the covers, and I recited the Lord's Prayer over and over again.

I felt something slip under the covers and my body went icy cold. "It's under the covers and on me!" I hysterically told Kath. We yanked the covers off of us, and as we did, the presence moved close to my face again. Now Kath was afraid. "Get out! Get out! Get out!" the voice bellowed in my ear.

I screamed again, and Kath and I bolted from the room. We ran downstairs and hid in the kitchen until 6.30 a.m. when Nicky walked in for her morning cup of tea. We threw ourselves on her and relayed our story.

"Oh, darling, I'm so sorry. I forgot to tell you that your room used to be the old nursery and it's haunted," Nicky informed us. She said that whenever children stayed in that room, they would say, "I don't mind the man visiting, but it would be nice if he put his head back on." Great! Thanks a lot! We refused to stay in that room again. The man may have liked children, but he hated young adults.

My first out-of-body experience happened in the manor a year later when I visited with my boyfriend. We were given a room in the attic, since I refused the nursery room due to my previous experience.

Before we went to bed, my boyfriend and I had an argument. He was not the type to brood and went straight to sleep. I, on the other hand, used to fret for ages and couldn't sleep. I sat cross-legged in bed, staring at the back of his head and trying to figure out how I could hit him without hurting him—an unlikely prospect, I know!

Whilst sulking, I heard a male voice repeatedly call my name. Then it said, "Samantha, it's time to go." I immediately left my body and levitated toward the ceiling, looking down upon myself. I noticed a thin, pulsating, silvery cord connecting my astral and physical bodies via the belly buttons.

The voice asked, "Are you ready? It's time to go." Still floating above my body, I looked to my left, since I could see something in my peripheral vision. A brilliant white light appeared to be coming from a tunnel. No one was there to greet me. Suddenly, I didn't want to go. I was too young to die and had too much to do. "No!" I replied, and with that I was transported straight back into my body.

When I became one with my body again, I hunkered down under the covers, grabbed my boyfriend's arm, and pulled it over my neck, as if this would prevent me from leaving my body again. I hadn't been drinking, I had never taken drugs, and I was very much awake when all of this had taken place. My mind went numb for days as I tried to figure out what had happened to me.

From that day on, I stopped spirit entities from speaking to me through their usual route and stuck to the traditional psychic means of my family. I am of Greek Cypriot heritage, and it is not unusual for us to "read" the Greek coffee cups. I had been doing this for years, so I continued to use that medium.

I shut down my gifts for good at thirty-one after our first child, Olivia, died during delivery. We found out that she had become sick during the pregnancy. I explain this in more detail in the chapter "The Divinity of the Soul."

In my grief and my anger at God, which came about six months after her funeral, I vowed never to give another person a message from "the other side," and I excommunicated myself from the Catholic faith and from God.

I was angry that such an innocent, pure little soul had been taken away from parents, who desperately wanted her when so many children were rejected by their parents and evil people were allowed to live. I became a staunch atheist, and whenever the opportunity arose, I would denigrate the so-called omnipresent God. I hated him and wanted nothing more to do with him.

My rage continued for the next nine years, and I filled my heart with the toxic waste of hatred.

The worm turned when I reached age forty and another dramatic and stressful period in my life ensued. I had received a phone call from a company claiming that I owed them thousands of dollars. I had never heard of them. My world was thrown into turmoil. I stopped eating, something I am prone to do when dealing with stress. The weight began falling off of me, and in one week I lost three kilograms. I was sixty kilograms and extremely lean to begin with, and as the weight kept dropping off, I began to look quite ill.

In October 2009, during a particularly stressful day when I had received another hideous phone call, I kept hearing the word *meditate*. Meditation, in my opinion, was for yogis, not for me, so I ignored the whispers in my ear. Then the word became louder and started sounding like a chant. After much resistance, I gave in, thinking, *What harm can it do?* I told my husband that I was going to the garden to try meditation.

It was the worst blind date of my life—with myself! The side of me that reared its head was utterly vile! It told me I was stupid, ugly, fat, deserved all I got, was unlovable, was a freak, and as predicted by schoolteachers, had never amounted to anything. The litany was viciously cruel! I sobbed and sobbed. When I emerged from the meditative state, I quietly said, "Oh my God! I really hate myself!"

I was heartbroken at my self-loathing.

Nick was appalled when I told him what had happened, and he asked how I was going to handle it. That simple question got my mind working overtime, and the next day I decided that I would try meditating again to see if this was an isolated incident. It wasn't. The monkey tongue of malicious intent ran riot on me. I was shellshocked again. Where did all this stem from?

Not one to back down from a challenge, I decided to find out. I began meditating twice a day for an hour each time. It was an emotionally draining experience, but over the course of six weeks the attacks slowed. I was shown pictures of my childhood, and memories began flooding back. Things I had placed in my mental safe box with the key thrown away were being revealed, forcing me to face my fears. By understanding their source, I began to heal from the inside out.

I started feeling strange sensations. The back of my tongue vibrated, and my palms heated up and tingled. What I now know as my base chakra also vibrated, and when I would come out of meditation, everything around me would oscillate, including the walls of my house. I saw red and blue orbs, and as they flew, some of them would settle by the ears of my husband and children.

I was convinced that my eyesight was failing and that I was going stark raving bonkers. I visited an optician and had my eyes thoroughly examined. I was given the all clear. Off to the doctor I went. I was fine. I saw a psychoanalyst. I was sane. So what on earth was wrong with me?

I kept up my meditation, and in November 2010, I had two poignant experiences.

The first occurred while I was meditating outside under my covered front porch on a rainy night. I suddenly felt myself being made to stand, as if hands under my armpits were forcing me upward. As I stood, my arms were lifted into the crucifix position and held there. I could not move them no matter how I tried. They were then moved to cross over my chest and pinned in position by what I could tell was someone else's arms. I then had the sensation of wings being wrapped around me. My body, not under my control, rocked to and fro.

I felt a hand reaching into my head through the crown area, moving all the way to my heart. Suddenly, my heart felt like someone had given it a squeeze. I thought I was suffering a heart attack and was convinced I was going to die. I was terrified.

A deep masculine voice just beside my right ear kept saying "Shh. You're safe. Nothing bad will happen. Have trust, little one." As he spoke, I felt myself being filled with a warm, loving energy, and my panic began to fade. A short while later, I felt incredibly calm.

After a while, the hand began withdrawing from my head, and I felt my body, mind, and heart become lighter. It was as if all my pain and sorrow were lifted right out of me. I began weeping for what I had lost. I felt my identity had been taken. I didn't know any other way of living my life. It was really frightening!

The voice spoke again, saying, "Hush. This is as it should be, child. To make way for your new life, your old heart had to be cleansed. Blessed be. Peace shall now come to you."

I knew deep within my new heart that I had been touched by what is traditionally known as the Holy Spirit and that the speaker was my guardian angel. Since that day, I have never looked back.

Although I have crossed swords with the spirits on occasion, no matter how often I churlishly threaten to close down again, they know I can't. I am a part of God as he/she is of me. That is something I cannot change.

The hatred that I had directed towards God had actually been received by the God essence lying within me. By hating God, I was hating myself. The poison of hatred filled me, going nowhere but inward. No wonder I was so miserable!

I felt free of the pain that I had been carrying.

The second event that completely blew me away came during a much-needed four-day family holiday spent on Daydream Island in mid-November 2010. I meditated each day, as was my custom. Our holiday was blissfully relaxing, and we simply enjoyed each other's company.

On the day we were to return to Melbourne, we had to fly out from Hamilton Island. As we were sitting in the airport lounge, I found myself staring out of the window at our airplane on the tarmac. I saw about a dozen grey oval shapes begin to form in the window. *Interesting,* I thought. *I wonder what they are.*

The shapes gathered into a single mass that covered the window. The mass turned a beautiful shade of pink and pulsated, growing larger and larger until it looked like a cloud. This cloud-like mass made its way to the plane and grew to such a size that the left side of the aircraft was covered. A circle formed in the middle of the cloud, and at its center appeared a white angel with no discernible facial features.

I was dumbfounded.

Once I managed to get my wits about me, I spoke to my husband. "Honey, what do you see when you look out the window?" I asked.

"A plane and blue sky," he responded. "Why?"

"Can't you see the pink cloud with an angel in the middle of it covering the plane?"

"What the hell are you talking about?" he retorted somewhat anxiously. I then turned my full attention on my husband. In the middle of his forehead, a third eye appeared, and it was green! I did a double take. I looked at my son, and he too had a third eye staring at me, but it was pink. My daughter's was yellow.

"Bloody hell, you've got three eyes! All of you do, and there's a pink cloud covering the plane with an angel in the middle of the cloud. What the hell is going on? Please tell me you can see what I'm seeing!" I exclaimed.

"Hon, keep your voice down. People are staring and they're going to think you're hallucinating!" said my ever-patient hubby.

"Maybe you're right. If the cloud has gone when we step out onto the tarmac, I'll know it was a figment of my imagination and I've been hallucinating," I agreed, and off we trundled towards the plane. I closed my eyes just before we stepped out onto the tarmac. I opened them again, looked up at the plane, and lo and behold the cloud was still there!

"Babe, it's still there! I'm not hallucinating!" I said. Then the angel in the cloud raised its hand, acknowledging my presence. Feeling like a nitwit, I waved back.

Before we climbed the stairs to embark, I watched the cloud get smaller and hover next to the first two passenger windows on the left side of the plane. We climbed the stairs and walked to our seats, which were situated exactly where the pink cloud was hovering by the first two passenger windows.

Well blow me down! I had asked for extra protection for our journey home (actually, it was more like a simple request that we get home safely), and here was an angel, showing me that we were being looked after.

I looked out of the window as the plane was ascending, and beside the wing were two rainbow-coloured winged beings waving at me. OK, so now I was certifiable!

I closed my eyes, and twenty minutes later I opened them and looked out of the window.

The two winged beings were still there. After much staring and not much thinking (my brain was too addled), I looked toward the sun, which was beginning to set. It was breathtakingly beautiful. Something drew my attention, and I looked in the opposite direction from the sun and saw another enormous sun-like orb filling the skyline. It was pure pink.

Confusing thoughts rushed into my head. *Well, that could be because the sun is setting. Hang on a second! There's only one sun! What the hell is that?*

This amazing sphere then simply vanished from my sight. I still don't know why I saw the orb, but it was awe-inspiring.

By this time, I was beginning to calm down and simply said thank you. To this day, I completely accept what I saw with my eyes wide open. I was not hallucinating, I am not batty, and I am most certainly not prone to flights of fancy.

My roller-coaster ride was not finished, I then experienced what I now know to be my own personal and spiritual transformation.

This strange phenomenon continued back in Melbourne. The sky would regularly turn from blue to pink and back again, and I would often see (via my peripheral vision) what I at first thought were shooting stars in the night sky. I would see these stars three or four times a night.

One evening while I sat in my backyard star gazing, an enormous electric-blue orb encircled by a clear white ring flew across the horizon right in my line of sight. I expected it to disappear like the shooting stars I had seen. The orb stopped in the distance, flashed three times, then vanished. A pure-white shooting star immediately followed. It was similar to the pulsating blue orb except for the colour and the fact that it didn't flash. It flew quickly to the place where the blue orb had been and stopped for a few seconds. Then it too disappeared. Neither the orb nor the shooting star had a tail.

I was seeing strange things in the night sky, and to this day I don't know what they were.

After these night-time occurrences, I found my daytime interactions with the spirit world picking up. It must have been decided that I wasn't paying enough attention.

One bright, sunny day I decided to do some writing whilst sitting at the garden table. I got pen and paper, and my husband made sure our children had plenty of food and entertainment for the next hour or so. About two pages into my writing, flying ants began falling on my pad. After a while, having brushed off many of the creatures from my work, I got up and irritatedly moved the table and chair to the other end of the yard. I settled back down to write. No sooner had I done so when the flying ants again began falling in droves. Normal people would have given up. Not I! Frustrated, I moved again to another part of the yard, but the flying ants kept falling. Now I noticed that they seemed to be in pairs, as if they were mating.

By this time, I was thoroughly irate. I looked above me and circling my head in a bright pink cloud that spun like a tornado were hundreds of flying ants that gave the appearance of dance partners.

"Fine. I get it!" I muttered. "Love is all around me. Can you cut that out so I can get on with my writing? Oh, and I love you, too!"

As soon as I acknowledged the message, the cloud disappeared and the flying ants dispersed, leaving me alone. It was made quite clear to me that day that if the spirits want your attention, they will do what is needed to get it.

I'm grateful that I have given myself permission to live. This has enabled me to see and feel extraordinary things. I no longer have a problem with being labelled odd. I have accepted the fact that I don't fit society's definition of normal and have embraced my peculiar status.

Interestingly, since I have made my true self known, many people have demanded that I prove the supernatural to them. They say they want to believe but need proof first. In truth, I can't prove anything to anyone. Proof comes during one's personal journey, and each person's truth will differ. Even if I could produce a Ferrari before someone's eyes, the person might still believe I had performed a trick, using distraction techniques.

Our truths can be revealed only when we are completely ready to see them not with our eyes, but with our hearts. Once this happens, our eyes can see beyond the veils that we perceive as reality.

I will never look at this great planet or the lives of human beings in the same way again. We are all so much more than we are led to believe, and the time for me to live my dream has begun.

The following chapters detail the processes that have brought me to self-realisation. During the last few years, I have learned to appreciate who and what I am outside of my physical being. I have accomplished this by learning as much as I could about the electromagnetic energy that surrounds all things animate and inanimate. I hope my experiences offer you some of the same understanding that my journey has brought me.

By allowing myself to be open to the extraordinary, I have exposed myself to a whole new world. Starting as a left-brained, analytical person, I have begun to awaken my right brain from its slumber and in doing so have discovered the reason I am here on earth. I have found my life path, and I feel complete.

I teach personal and spiritual development classes, and although I occasionally give psychic medium readings, my true passion is motivating and assisting people to find their life paths. I get enormous pleasure from watching people grow into the very best they can be. Shy individuals have found their voice. Underachievers have begun achieving beyond what they thought possible. I watch people's eyes light up when they know in which direction to walk.

Although I have made it my philosophy not to teach anything that I have not experienced for myself, I am more than happy to hear how others have realised their own truths and will try out these techniques for myself. All the chapters that follow are about my voyage of self-discovery both as a human and as a spiritual being.

This book is about my journey into the unknown.

The Divinity of the Soul

Before discussing the divinity of the soul, I would like to note that I refer to the Creator as God and describe God by using the male gender. Although I know that God is neither male nor female, it feels wrong to refer to him as an it, for an it is inanimate, and God most certainly is not inanimate.

Feel free to change my word to what feels comfortable to you—for example, great spirit, creator, all that is, or goddess.

Now I wish to pose a question to ponder for a moment. What does your soul mean to you?

Is this an open question? Perhaps, but the answer will be unique to you. As your soul speaks, universal truths that are yours alone reveal themselves. These truths include your loves, likes, dislikes, fears, and beliefs. Your soul is like a radio transmitter, emitting sounds and colourful energy at its own frequency, and it is quite unlike any other person's. It allows you to experience life and living in a way unique to you.

We may have similar experiences, though my experiences will vary slightly from yours. However, in those differences I get the opportunity to add to my stockpile of understanding by listening to what has happened to you.

So what does my soul mean to me? I now share with you information that I have been blessed to receive in discussions with my own soul, a soul linked to the one consciousness. I am a multifaceted and utterly unique individual.

Your soul comes encoded with the information you need to succeed on your journey of learning. You can succeed by experiencing every facet of life in the form you have chosen. You are already equipped

13

with all the tools you need to travel on your great adventure. The question is why so many incredible beings struggle as they do, unable to decide which direction to take. Perhaps they are overcome by a sense of abandonment or loneliness at stages of their lives.

If we have the tools, how is it that we not know what to do? This is the question that millions before us have asked and that millions after us may pose. So if humanity remains baffled by this enigma, why hasn't someone found the answer? Well someone has, and that someone is you! How is that so?

Drawing on my humble understanding of what I have learned to be my own truth, I will try to explain what lay dormant within me but rose to the surface through self-reflection.

Surely you have at some point faced a decision that would have an enormous impact on your life or on the lives of people for whom you cared deeply. Confronting this decision, you may have had a strong feeling in your gut that said, *No, not that way* or *Don't do that.* Alternatively, your gut instinct may have said, *Yes, that's it. This feels right.* You have listened, and the outcome was what you hoped for. You unconsciously tapped into the great reservoir of the wise, ageless, limitless being that you are. You delved into your bottomless well of knowledge and lifted out exactly what you required in your time of need. No matter how big or small the decision, you should view the action you took with great pride.

I endured this situation when faced with the death of my daughter. The decision my husband and I made was the most selfless act of love a parent can offer a child.

In 2000, I was pregnant with our first child, and during one of the ultrasounds at the end of the second trimester, we found out that our baby was sick. We had more ultrasounds and an amniocentesis. In this procedure, a big needle is put through the abdomen into the uterus to get a sample of amniotic fluid. It is an accurate way of diagnosing the condition of babies still in the womb.

The results were heartbreaking. Our baby had less than a 5 percent chance of survival. Our world fell apart. My husband and I were given three choices, all of which had the same outcome.

Death for Olivia.

We went away and spent the next two weeks with our little angel. My husband and I could not change the outcome, but we could change how we dealt with it and make it easier for her and for us. We talked to her, sang to her, and became one with her.

As Olivia's mother, I particularly felt the union of our souls. They linked with the consciousness from which we came, and in the deep communication that occurred, my soul awakened from its slumber and spoke.

I was to set her free, and in coming to that realisation I felt my body fill with love. A love I never knew could exist. A love I could do no justice if I attempted to put it into words now.

I knew that the unconditional love for our baby girl was coming from somewhere else and from something else. It was so pure and so devoid of any human qualities, and I knew she would be looked after on the other side. So we let her go. We returned her to her maker, freeing her to be the divine being she is.

We knew it would be selfish to keep her here, so we released her with our love into the hands of God, her true parent. We searched our inner library of truth and knew that what we were doing was for the greater good.

After many years of grief and anger over the loss of Olivia, which I now realise were part of the mourning process, I was touched by the Holy Spirit. This changed me to such a degree that I have no regrets about that great tragedy. Even though I had been angry, I never doubted our decision or the existence of God (even though I had become an atheist of sorts). I was simply furious with him. However, I have always felt that we were blessed to have Olivia in our lives for a short while, and that is something I would never want to change. Of course we miss her, but I am proud that we drew on our divine love and did what was right for our little girl.

How was I able to do it? How were you able to make your own life-changing decisions? How were you able to trust your instincts? Consciously or unconsciously, you knew that as a limitless, unique being as individual as your thumb print, a being born from the one that created us all aeons ago, you could draw on the knowledge already lying within you to bring about the outcome, whatever it might be.

This is the knowledge that God offers you as his child, and as a child of the divine you too are divine and have divine knowledge from which to draw.

Unfortunately, we often become disconnected from the grace of our inner truth and become immersed in the drama of our daily lives. We lose the part of ourselves that connects so easily to the God spark that is our spirit, making our journey that much more difficult.

In one of the many interactions that I have had in discovering my inner truth, the powers that be and my soul allowed me insight that changed my way of thinking. I hope this truth has the same impact on you. In this enlightening moment when I had opened myself completely to communications from above and within, I learned that humans are shackled by their sense of worth. That worth is determined by the beliefs others imposed on us during our tender childhood years.

But a child born from the eternal, unconditional flame of love is created as a perfect being of light. God, the parent of this child, sees only with loving eyes. As his perfect creation, you hold within you all there is in God. Only you who know your true worth can give or take from your being. You hold the courage within to unlock the chains that may bind you and to allow yourself the freedom that is yours by divine birthright.

In your inner sanctum is the very heart of everything you look for in life. It is there that you will find peace, understanding, compassion, acceptance, learning, truth, and most important of all, unconditional love.

Recognise your inner identity with the divine and realise that in your soul you are identical to God. In your soul, you are one with the divine in all circumstances, good or bad.

Your true reality is a boundless, all-seeing, all-hearing, all-feeling intelligence. It reacts to everything, witnesses everything, and is able to communicate with you, protect you, and enlighten you, enabling you to sense your oneness with divine perfection. This formless form knows no time, space, or bounds. It is endless perfection, absolute love, absolute wisdom, absolute life. It is eternal. It is immortal. It is you.

The universe is an extension of yourself because you are part of the one that created it. When you ask God for help, forgiveness, answers, even for that elusive lottery win, you are in fact addressing the very God essence that is part of your unique soul blueprint. It is right there at your fingertips and in your heart, so you should not feel guilty about tapping into your own essence.

Mankind and God are one, experiencing all the positives and negatives together. This is our reality.

As soon as the soul becomes incarnate in the form of a human body, it forgets its origin and becomes confused. It enters into a state much like sleepwalking. It loses its boundless joy and contentment. It is no longer consciously linked with the divine but with the world of the senses. In such a state, it is difficult to identify with God. The senses misguide us and reveal only a false, illusionary world. Yet God is always present in the divinity of our souls.

Those who doubt that they are one with God often feel fearful, separated, and unconnected to the whole. They are not in alignment with their divine origin, and their doubt keeps them alienated.

Our source is God, the very essence of our being. God is celestial and beyond us, yet he is within us.

When you relinquish your human attachment to logical thinking and allow yourself to feel as your soul, this concept is no longer confusing.

Many people tell me that only God is perfect or that there is no such thing as perfection. I disagree. Who decided what was or was not perfect? Mankind did, not God! Absolutely, God is perfect, but every person reading this, every unique soul holding this book, is a spark of divine love and light and thus is perfect, too. My personal truth, which I accept with my whole heart, tells me that our parent, God, believes this. God wants you to believe in yourself and to believe that you are worthy of all things bright and beautiful. You are holy and divine. Believe it! I do!

That is not to say that times do not occasionally get tough, but when you acknowledge and accept what you are, these times do not feel quite so lonely.

You have God's genes within you, and if you accept who you are, perhaps against the wishes of those who would oppress you, your challenges will become less difficult. The universe will deliver to you what you need, because the universe lies within you. Here your toolbox is stored, waiting to be used.

Remember your own divinity. You are a unique individual, a limitless being.

I wrote a poem that I would like to share. I hope it has as much meaning for you as it has for me.

Immortality of Time

The past does not exist, for it is time elapsed.
The future does not exist, for it is time yet to be.
Only the present exists, for the now essence
is the one true aspect of time.
Learn from the past.
Plan for the future.
Live only in the now.

By accepting who you truly are, you will live in the now as God does, and you will allow yourself to accomplish all those things you believed were impossible. By focussing on another person's dreams, you take time away from your own. Give yourself permission to live your dream, and watch it come true.

Here is a mantra I chant every day, perhaps three to four times a day. It makes me feel wonderful and reminds me of my inner divine spark.

I am the soul.
I am the light divine.
I am love.
I am will.
I am final design.
I am a child of the light,
Walking in the light,
Working with the light,
A being of light.
And as a being of light,
May the light within me shine forth for all to see
So that they too may be attracted to the light,

To begin their journey to become one with the light.
Everything I do is for the greater good of all.
So be it.

Close your eyes and ask your soul to make itself known to you. Feel your soul move in your body, filling you with its light. Ask your soul to speak to you. Ask it to reveal its God spark in all its glorious beauty. Ask your soul what it knows to be your dreams, and ask for those dreams to be made manifest in your world.

What I have written here is my truth, and my truth alone. I do not profess to know what truths lie within you. All I can hope for is that some of what I have written resonates with you. If it does, take this learning that has helped me understand what I was looking for and incorporate some or all of it into your own journey.

SPIRITUAL AWARENESS

Spiritual awareness comes from a transformation that has occurred within you. It does not require a profound, life-altering experience, although this may be the case for some.

This transformation comes about when you pay attention to your thoughts, feelings, and behaviours. I call it becoming consciously aware of the unconscious, or conscious awareness of the known unknown.

As you do this, your identification with yourself shifts from who you think you are to who you really are. It is extraordinary how the simple act of paying attention to your thoughts, feelings, and behaviours allows you to see who you really are and what you need to modify or eliminate. When you pay attention, you find that your consciousness effortlessly awakens to authentic spiritual growth and spiritual transformation.

The act of self-observation allows you to step back from yourself, enabling you to shift from the sense that your thoughts, feelings, and behaviours define who you are to a new view that permits you to understand that you are simply having those thoughts, feelings, and behaviours. They are passing emotional, mental, and physical responses that vary from moment to moment depending on the stimulus encountered.

Previous perceptions of yourself give way to the authenticity of your constant sense of self—your pure, observing higher awareness. As you shift into a higher level of consciousness, you will begin to see the world through the eyes of your God essence and not through the eyes of your feelings, behaviours, and thoughts.

Self-awareness encourages the knowledge that you are not your thoughts and feelings. You are, in fact, an ageless and wise being, and over time, this truth has the power to change your life. Awareness of this truth usually brings a great calm and inner peace.

The feeling can be described as a sense of belonging, an acceptance of who you are, and the understanding of self. Spiritual awareness makes you feel complete, in the sense that you understand who you are beyond your physical body.

A spiritual transformation means:

1. A shift has occurred, moving you away from indoctrination by others, which generally happens when your spirituality is connected to a religious belief system. The shift directs you towards a more authentic spirituality based on your personal truths and experiences, not what you have been taught to believe.
2. Your self-identity has become less emotionally linked to your primitive desires and fears. When this happens, your need for power or control over others leaves you.
3. You are in alignment with your observing consciousness and the spiritual ideals of connectedness and collaboration.
4. You have moved closer to knowing who you really are, a truth found at a deeper level of your psyche.
5. Your desire to help humanity rises to the surface as you realise that we are all connected to each other.

As you come to realise that your pure observing consciousness is the same consciousness that others experience, you may feel an overpowering sense of responsibility for the forms you create, based on the understanding that creation of all matter is led by pure consciousness.

When you become aware of your higher consciousness, you recognise that your observing consciousness is the same as that of the Creator. You will begin to acknowledge that you too are holy and divine, a co-creator working alongside the Creator through the astonishing, eternal process of evolution that created and is continuously changing the universe.

CHAKRAS

Before you can understand what a chakra is and the role it plays in your body and your life, it is important to be aware of a number of features relating to the body, including *prana,* and their significance to your functioning.

When you begin developing your awareness outside of the five senses you are accustomed to working with, a new world reveals itself to you. This hidden world was always there but was invisible until you began tapping into it.

As your consciousness heightens and your thoughts and feelings come to light, you may become more acquainted with sides of your environment and your life that you have never noticed before. They may reveal themselves in a kaleidoscope of colours and shapes that you never thought possible.

The human body is a wondrous miracle of creation, with far more to it than just the physical aspect. Sadly, many people consider the physical side and the material world to be the only reality. This is understandable, since this is the only certainty that they have experienced. Therefore they believe what they see, feel, taste, smell, and hear with their five physical senses. These are the only things that can be recognised and understood by the rational mind, which is controlled by the analytical left side of the brain.

The right side of the brain controls our creativity and our ability to see beyond the five material senses. Unfortunately, as a species, we have been trained not to trust the right side of the brain (affected on an unconscious level), and as a result, during our evolution we have become left brain-oriented. Should we wish to explore ourselves and our being further, we must realise that there are numerous energy bodies within and around the human body and that each energy body holds its own vibration frequency, from the densest (etheric body: base/root chakra) to the finest (ketheric body: crown chakra). These energy bodies are listed below:

1. Etheric Body: Corresponds with the base/root chakra and extends a quarter inch to two inches from the body.

2. Emotional Body: Corresponds with the sacral chakra and extends one to three inches from the body.

3. Mental Body: Corresponds with the solar plexus chakra and extends three to eight inches from the body.

4. Astral Body: Corresponds with the heart chakra and extends six to twelve inches from the body.

5. Etheric Template: Corresponds with the throat chakra and extends twelve to twenty-four inches from the body.

6. Celestial Body: Corresponds with the brow/third eye chakra and extends twenty-four to thirty-five inches from the body.

7. Ketheric Body: Corresponds with the crown chakra and extends thirty-five to forty-six inches from the body.

There is also a complex energy system at work, one that the body requires to exist. These energy bodies are nadis (energy channels) and chakras (energy centres).

What Is Nadi?

Nadi is a Sanskrit[1] word meaning "pipe" or "vein." Nadis are connected to a system of pathways or arteries that carry prana (the life-giving force) throughout a body's energy system.

---

[1] Sanskrit is an ancient Indian language, considered to be the oldest language in the world, with examples of Vedic Sanskrit dating back to around 1500 BC. The language is made up of basic sounds arranged to include the natural tones created by the human mouth.

According to ancient Indian texts, there are seventy-two thousand nadis in the human body; other texts say there are 350,000. No matter how many there are, the nadis of one energy body are thought to be connected to the nadis of the adjacent energy body by way of chakras.

What Is Prana?

Prana is the primordial source of all forms of energy and manifests itself in a variety of vibrations. The Western world identifies it as the life-giving force, and it is within you and all around you.

One aspect of prana is your ability to breathe and to eat, and by doing what comes naturally, you draw into yourself a part of prana from the air and from food. This is essential to your existence.

Prana generally cannot be seen with the naked eye, but just because we cannot see prana does not mean that it does not exist. Simply look at the miracle of the world around you. You will be unable to come up with a logical, scientific reason for its existence. Every thought, word, breath, and movement of life that we see has come about as a result of prana.

Your level of self-awareness determines the different frequencies of prana that you can receive, accumulate, and therefore incorporate into your body.

How Is Prana Distributed in the Body?

Humans are made up of atoms, and we need to absorb oxygen, water, and food (which are also made up of atoms) into our bodies to survive. The health of the body on all levels dictates how much prana we can take into our bodies and energy fields. The prana is then filtered through our chakras before being passed on to the rest of the body. An unhealthy body might be more likely to have a poor aura and blocked chakras, which takes more energy to clear and balance.

If you think of how red blood cells work, this process might be easier to understand. The red blood cells' primary function is to carry oxygen throughout the body, moving through the respiratory system to collect oxygen, then travelling through the blood vessels to other tissues in the body. Red blood cells also remove carbon dioxide and other impurities from the body. The energies in the human energy field absorb and carry energy, or prana, from the atmosphere, disposing of unwanted material in a very similar way.

What Are Chakras?

Chakra is a Sanskrit word meaning "wheel." Chakras are spinning, wheel-like whirlpools of energy that exist in and on the surface of the body. For the most part, they are not visible to the naked eye. They extend from the front, back, top, and bottom of the body.

There are thought to be eighty-eight thousand chakras in the body. Most are very small and play a minor role in its energy system. There are also roughly forty significant secondary chakras—for example, those located in the palms of your hands and the soles of your feet.

To avoid confusion and information overload, we will only explore the seven primary chakras, which are the main energy centres that exist from the top of the head down through the spinal column to the groin area.

Through the nadis, the chakras take in fundamental energy and convert it into vibrations required by different areas of the body for growth and nourishment.

Chakras are shaped like funnels, and they extend from your spine forward, backward, upward, and downward through and out of your body to about twenty centimeters.

These circular energy centres are constantly rotating, perpetually attracting or expending energy. The stem of each chakra is like a canal that extends to the spine and connects the chakra with the crown chakra. The spinal column acts as a channel. This process allows you to have divine communication with your higher self and with the one consciousness. I have found that the crown chakra is the easiest to see. When I first saw mine, it appeared to be shaped like the mouth of a trumpet, was lilac in colour, and had a spinning golden orb of energy in the middle. This is how my crown chakra still appears today.

Chakras can function at varying levels. When open, they are considered normal, healthy, and balanced. In an ideal world, they would all work in perfect harmony, contributing to our health and well-being. Unfortunately, this is not often the case; some are underactive (not open enough) and some may be overactive (too open). When chakras are overactive, they are most often overcompensating for the underactive ones, and the underactive ones must be stimulated to function correctly.

The Seven Major Human Chakras

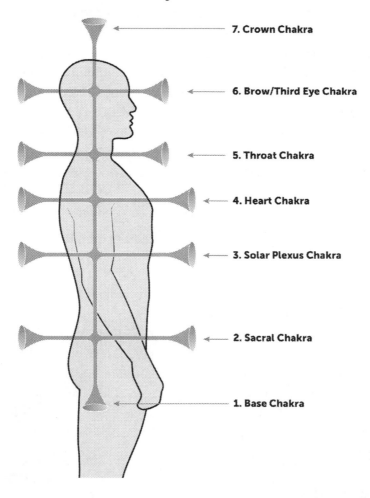

7. Crown Chakra

6. Brow/Third Eye Chakra

5. Throat Chakra

4. Heart Chakra

3. Solar Plexus Chakra

2. Sacral Chakra

1. Base Chakra

What Are the Names of Chakras and What Are Their Functions?

First Chakra—Base or Root

The base chakra represents life-force energy and gives vitality to the body, aids in self-preservation, and supplies instincts.

The base chakra is located between the anus and the genitals (testicles for males and perineum for females) and is connected to the coccyx. This chakra opens downward between the legs and is symbolised by four petals.

Colour: Red (secondary, black)

Aura Layer Link: Etheric body

Responds to: Yang (masculine influence) and musical note C

Glands and Organs: Adrenals, kidneys, spinal column, colon, legs, and bones

Gems and Minerals: Ruby, garnet, bloodstone, red jasper, black tourmaline, obsidian, smoky quartz, and hematite

Foods: Red fruits and vegetables, proteins. However, meat and dairy foods are not recommended when trying to balance the base chakra.

Positive Qualities: When this chakra is balanced, material and physical needs are met. You will find yourself grounded, stable, secure, patient, and healthy. You will feel physically at one with yourself and have a sense of belonging and being at home in situations.

Negative Qualities: When the base chakra is unbalanced, there is a tendency towards self-centeredness, materialism, greed, violence, anger, obsession with feeling secure, and excessive concern with one's survival. Physical manifestations of an unbalanced base chakra are tension in the spine and constipation.

If you tend to feel nervous or fearful or suffer paranoia, you may find your base chakra is underactive.

If you are often excessively aggressive or violent, you may find this chakra is overactive.

Second Chakra—Sacral

The sacral chakra represents creativity, reproduction, food absorption, sexuality, physical power, and vitality.

It is located in the lower abdomen, two fingers' width below the navel, and is symbolised by six petals.

Colour: Orange

Aura Layer Link: Emotional body

Responds to: Yang (masculine influence) and musical note D

Glands and Organs: Ovaries, womb, testicles, prostate, genitals, spleen, and bladder

Gems and Minerals: Carnelian, coral, gold calcite, amber, citrine, gold topaz, and peach aventurine

Foods: Orange foods and vegetables

Positive Qualities: When this chakra is balanced, you feel in control and have healthy self-esteem. You experience a free flow of feelings and can express yourself without being overly emotional. You are capable of working harmoniously and creatively with others, are open to intimacy, and can be energetic and enthusiastic. You have no problems dealing with or accepting your sexuality.

Negative Qualities: When the sacral chakra is unbalanced, there is a tendency towards possessiveness, confusion, jealousy, envy, a feeling of being worthless and without purpose, and overindulgence in food or sex. Physical manifestations of an unbalanced sacral chakra are sexual difficulties and uterine and/or bladder problems.

If you tend to be rigid or to have an unemotional face, then the sacral chakra is most likely underactive.

If you tend to be emotional most of the time, have excessive emotional attachment to people, and are very sexual, then the sacral chakra may be overactive.

Third Chakra—Solar Plexus

The solar plexus chakra represents will power, personal power, authority, energy, mastery of desire, self-control, radiance, warmth, transformation, joy, sympathy, aspirations, and emotional identification.

This chakra is also concerned with extrasensory energies that involve paranormal phenomena.

It is located above the navel and below the chest in the area where the ribs meet, and is symbolised by ten petals.

Colour: Yellow

Aura Layer Link: Mental body

Responds to: Yang (masculine influence) and musical note E

Glands and Organs: Pancreas, adrenals, stomach, liver, gallbladder, nervous system, and muscles

Gems and Minerals: Citrine, gold topaz, amber, tiger eye, gold calcite, and gold

Foods: Yellow fruits and vegetables, grains, and fibre

Positive Qualities: When this chakra is balanced, you will have a sense of self-worth and the ability to be confident and in control of your life.

Negative Qualities: When the solar plexus chakra is unbalanced, there is a tendency towards taking in more that you can assimilate and therefore use. There is anger, fear, and hate, and too much emphasis on power and/or recognition. Physical manifestations of an unbalanced solar plexus chakra are digestive problems, ulcers, diabetes, hypoglycaemia, constipation, nervousness, toxicity, parasites, colitis, and poor memory.

        If you have a tendency to be passive and indecisive, then your solar plexus chakra is most likely underactive.

        If you have a tendency to be domineering and aggressive, then this chakra may be overactive.

Fourth Chakra—Heart

The heart chakra represents the higher emotions, which are divine and unconditional love, compassion, sympathy, forgiveness, understanding, group consciousness, acceptance, peace, openness, harmony, and contentment.

It is located in the centre of the chest above the solar plexus and is symbolised by twelve petals.

Colour: Green (secondary, pink)

Aura Layer Link: Astral body

Responds to: Yin and yang (feminine and masculine influences of perfect balance) and musical note F

Glands and Organs: Heart, thymus gland, circulatory system, arms, hands, lungs, and chest

Gems and Minerals: Emerald, green and pink tourmaline, malachite, green jade, green aventurine, chrysoprase, kunzite, rose quartz, and ruby

Foods: Green fruits and vegetables

Positive Qualities: When this chakra is balanced, you are compassionate, friendly, and work in harmonious relationships.

Negative Qualities: When the heart chakra is unbalanced, there is a tendency to repress love, to feel out of balance, and to suffer emotional instability. Physical manifestations of an unbalanced heart chakra are heart and circulatory issues.

If you are inclined to be cold and distant, then your heart chakra is most likely underactive.

If you tend to suffocate people with your love and are needy in relationships, then this chakra may be overactive.

Fifth Chakra—Throat

The throat chakra represents communication and the power of the spoken word, creative communication in the arts, and peace, truth, knowledge, wisdom, sound, and rhythm.

It is located in the nook of the neck at the front and is symbolised by sixteen petals.

Colour: Sky blue

Aura Layer Link: Etheric template

Responds to: Yin (feminine influence) and musical note G

Glands and Organs: Thyroid, parathyroid, hypothalamus, throat, and mouth

Gems and Minerals: Turquoise, chrysocolla, celestite, blue topaz, sodalite, lapis lazuli, aquamarine, azurite, kyanite, and blue lace agate

Foods: Blue or purple fruits and vegetables

Positive Qualities: When this chakra is balanced, you are able to express yourself in a kind, compassionate, and truthful way.

Negative Qualities: When the throat chakra is unbalanced, there is a tendency to have communication problems and speech impediments, to be ignorant, and to gossip. Physical manifestations of an unbalanced throat chakra are depression and thyroid problems.

If you are inclined to be introverted and shy, then the throat chakra is most likely underactive.

If you tend to talk too much, usually in a domineering way, or are a bad listener, then this chakra may be overactive.

Sixth Chakra—Brow or Third Eye

The brow or third eye chakra represents intuition, psychic abilities, vision, increased understanding, greater imagination, and the ability to easily overcome fears.

It is located in the centre of the forehead between and just above the eyebrows, and it is symbolised by two petals.

Colour: Indigo (dark blue)

Aura Layer Link: Celestial body

Responds to: Yin (feminine influence) and musical note A

Glands and Organs: Pituary gland, pineal gland, left eye, nose, and ears

Gems and Minerals: Lapis lazuli, azurite, sodalite, quartz crystal, sapphire, indicolite tourmaline, and amethyst

Foods: Blue or purple fruits and vegetables

Positive Qualities: When this chakra is balanced, you will have good insight with the ability to visualise.

Negative Qualities: When the brow chakra is unbalanced, you may not be very good at thinking for yourself and have to rely on other people. Physical manifestations of an unbalanced brow chakra are fear, cynicism, tension, headaches, eye troubles, bad dreams, lack of concentration, and being overly detached from the world.

If you are inclined to be rigid in your thinking and get confused easily, then the brow chakra is most likely underactive.

If you tend to excessively daydream and live in a world of fantasy, then this chakra may be overactive.

Seventh Chakra—Crown

The crown chakra represents the energy centre for all higher spiritual functions and growth, wisdom, inspiration, and meditation. It is considered to be the doorway between our spirit and the higher realms.

The crown chakra is the entrance for energy to the six previously mentioned chakras. If this chakra suffers a blockage, then the rest of the body and spirit is believed to suffer.

It is located on the top of the head and is symbolised by one thousand petals.

Colour: Violet, white, or gold

Aura Layer Link: Ketheric body

Responds to: Yin (feminine influence) and musical note B

Glands and Organs: Pineal gland, cerebral cortex, central nervous system, and right eye

Gems and Minerals: Amethyst, alexandrite, diamond, sugilite, purple fluorite, quartz crystal, selenite, and gold

Foods:　　　　　　　Purple or violet fruits and vegetables. However, this chakra is associated with fasting.

Positive Qualities:　When this chakra is balanced, you are at one with the world, are free of prejudice, nonjudgemental, and have good self-awareness.

Negative Qualities:　When the crown chakra is unbalanced, there is a tendency to be confused, depressed, and alienated, to lack inspiration, and to be reluctant to serve humanity. Physical manifestations of an unbalanced crown chakra are headaches, migraines, nervous system issues, amnesia, and eye problems.

　　　　　　　　　　　If you are particularly rigid in your way of thinking, then the crown chakra is most likely underactive.

　　　　　　　　　　　If you tend to intellectualise too much, are addicted to spirituality, are unaware of the world around you, and are ignoring your physical needs, then this chakra may be overactive.

MEDITATION

Meditation leads to a state of consciousness that brings clarity, peace, contentment, and self-realisation. The act of meditating produces a stillness that enables the mind and the body to relax and rejuvenate.

Why Meditate?

Human beings are constantly at the mercy of negative forces such as fear, anger, jealousy, doubt, worry, anxiety, and stress.

These energies are like leeches. They take from us what they need, never giving back. When they are full, they rest for a short while, and we get a small taste of peace. But not for long. When they get hungry again, they begin feeding off of our energy, taking our valuable life force, and the process starts over again.

To counteract these negative influences, meditation teaches us to centre ourselves and gain an understanding of why we react as we do in certain situations, enabling us to discover ways to more effectively and efficiently deal with problems.

When we begin this process through meditation and put what we have learned into practice, we release blockages in our physical and etheric bodies, and our vibration increases. When these blockages (also known as fears) are released, we connect to our higher selves and enter a state of peace.

How Will Meditation Help Me Grow Personally and Spiritually?

As you become more proficient at silencing the mind and stilling the body, you will find yourself delving deep into your inner world. While there, you will see, hear, feel, taste, and sense aspects of yourself that you may not previously have recognised. You will be shown truths to ponder, and when you take the time for contemplation, other aspects of self will emerge. As each side of your identity is acknowledged and validated, the amalgamation of your human self and spiritual self will commence.

By becoming more aware of your thoughts and actions, you realise your responsibility for determining your life and become accountable for the part you play in any situation. You begin to understand the action-equals-reaction theory.

This theory is based upon the simple principle that the reactions you draw from others reflect how you have been heard.

We communicate mostly by body language (55 percent of the time) and tone of voice (38 percent of the time). Only a small proportion of the words we use are heard. That is because we are bombarded by a staggering 2 million bytes of information per second, and though our brains can hold more, they have been conditioned to retain only 134 bytes per second. We must filter the events in our lives through our conscious and unconscious minds before we give them meaning. We are also more likely to focus on negative information, filtering out the positive.

As you develop, you will become more aware of how you interact with others in every phase of life, and the beauty of developing on a spiritual level is a more profound understanding of what your spirit, or divine self, can offer you.

You become aware of a shift in reality as you perceive it, and other worlds open themselves to you. Your heart feels lighter, less encumbered by the daily dramas of life, and you are able to see life through your divine eyes. As you develop, your connection to the God essence within strengthens, and you see and feel things in a nonjudgemental, accepting, compassionate, and loving way. Forgiving becomes easier, and so blockages are released or prevented. You can speak your truth in loving ways, and lying to yourself becomes impossible. You will live entirely in the truth of your reality as the unique individual that you are, no longer encumbered by the beliefs or actions of others. You will find the meaning of true freedom.

Life at times will throw you a curve ball or two, but when you think, feel, and act as your spirit self, you will find that the curve ball loses its impact and can be handled more easily.

Often when faced with difficult situations, I have found that once I take a moment to observe my behaviour (before my knee-jerk responses kick in), I manage to ask, *What would my higher self say or do right now?* When I do this, I usually find that I am filled with peace and understanding and can calmly deal with the issue. It is now extremely rare for me to overreact as I once did. Even so, when I do react excessively, I do not berate myself. I accept responsibility for my actions (right or wrong) and look for the lesson I need to learn from the incident.

Through introspection, I have found that any event can be turned into a tool for my personal development.

How Do I Meditate?

First, you must make time to meditate. Many people say they do not have time, but you can meditate in the shower or the bath or turn off the television and set aside fifteen minutes a day.

The effects of meditation are most noticeable when you do it regularly. You may like to end the day by clearing your mind, or you may prefer to meditate in the middle of the day. However, many people say that the easiest time to meditate is in the morning before the day gives you plenty to think about. It is up to you to determine the time of day that best suits your needs.

Here are basic instructions on how to begin meditating.

1. Find a quiet area in your house. It is extremely important, particularly as a novice, to avoid distractions such as televisions, phones, or other noisy appliances. If you play music, make sure it is calming and repetitive. Meditating outside is fine as long as you are not sitting near sources of loud noise such as a main road.

2. Make sure you are comfortable. Sit on the ground, a mat, a cushion, or a chair. It is important to keep your spine straight. If lying on the ground helps, that's great. However, the chance of falling asleep increases if you lie down.

3. Slowly straighten your spine, imagining your vertebrae are sitting perfectly aligned on top of one another. This exercise is intended to ensure that your spinal column is balanced enough to support the whole weight of your torso, head, and neck.

4. Close your eyes and try to relax completely. Focus the thought that you are relaxed on your feet and slowly work your way up your body to the top of your head, not forgetting your arms and legs.

5. Focus your attention on your breathing. The aim is to allow the dialogue in your mind to fade away. You may find it easier to count your breaths.

6. If you are struggling to keep your eyes closed, then you may want to begin with a focussed, open-eyed meditation. Light an unscented candle on a table in front of you and direct your attention to the flame. You will be surprised at how quickly the gentle, mesmerising movement of the flame transfixes you and how your mind empties itself. Keep your attention on the flame and feel your body and mind relaxing.

7. Another method is to recite a mantra. You can chant a traditional word like *om* at a steady rhythm or try a word like *relax* if you prefer. You can recite it out loud or say it in your mind.

8. Once you can focus on one thing, the next step is to place your attention on nothing at all. Clearing your mind requires discipline. If you concentrate on a single point and find that a thought or image presents itself, you can discard it or observe it with detachment, without labelling it as good or bad.

The important thing is not to give up if you are unable to sit still for fifteen minutes a day. Meditation takes practice and perseverance, but it offers astounding benefits once you can relax and do it for half an hour or more.

Guide and Guardian Spirits

Your personal philosophy will determine your view on spirit guides and guardians. Some believe that they do not exist and that all aspects of guidance come from your higher self—the being connected to you because it is you—and the universal consciousness. Others believe that numerous noncorporeal entities assist us throughout our lives on our spiritual journeys.

I will concentrate on the latter belief system. However, no matter what your dogma, continue with it if it feels right to you. One person's views are no more valued than another's. Your experiences and inner truths are what is most important.

What Are Spirit Guides and Guardians?

Spirit guides and guardians are nonphysical beings who accompany you through an incarnation and help teach you the lessons you agreed to learn before your birth.

Some guides stay with you throughout your life, whilst others may help at stages and then leave. These guides are at different levels of their own development and consciousness and may have had physical incarnations themselves.

When the time comes for you to begin fulfilling your earthly mission, they tune in to your energy vibrations so that they can provide guidance.

Your guides will always use uplifting, gentle, and loving words. They will never disparage or judge you. If what you are saying or doing is harmful, they will gently show you how you might speak or act in a kinder or better way. They will never reprimand you or give you illusions of grandeur. They will endeavour to balance the spiritual and earthly aspects of your life. If you feel you are the target of reproach or criticism, your own inner dialogue (superego) is running rampant. Incidentally, I believe that the inner dialogue is not the ego, as we have been led to believe, but the superego, and that *ego* is not a bad word.

I have listed below the three main components of self (according to Sigmund Freud[2]) so that you can gain a greater understanding of your inner dialogue. Many assume this to be bad spirits at play. That can happen, of course, but generally it is the darker, more critical side of ourselves at work.

Id, Ego, and Superego

Id: The id is the child within and is an important part of our personality because as newborns, it allows us to have our basic needs met. The id is based on our pleasure principle. It wants whatever feels good at the time, with no thought for the situation.

When a child is hungry, the id wants food, and so the child cries. If the child needs to be changed, the id relays the demand. When the child is uncomfortable, in pain, too hot, too cold, or just wants attention, the id speaks up until the child's needs are met.

Ego: The ego is our sense of self and is based on the reality principle. The ego understands that other people have needs and desires and that sometimes being impulsive or selfish can hurt us in the long run. It is the ego's job to

---

[2]   There is continuing debate on the three aspects of self. Some believe that they are all housed in the ego, whilst others think that the superego does not exist. The three listed have resonated with me, enabling me to start understanding my inner self. However, it may be different for you.

meet the needs of the id, taking into consideration the reality of the situation.

Superego: Most of the superego is formed during our upbringing. Our parents teach us what is right and wrong, what we should and should not do, what is normal and what is not.

We may be forced to accept rules in subtle and not-so-subtle ways such as punishment, public shaming, or ridicule for doing something wrong.

Besides our parents, many people in our early environment pressure us to abide by rules. Adults in positions of authority (such as government officials, religious leaders, and schoolteachers) become part of our superego's conditioning. So do other children. A Chinese proverb says that a child's life is like a piece of paper on which every person leaves a mark.

In adulthood, we continue to pressure each other when we act out our superegos.

The superego is the sum of all the people who have tried to make us behave according to certain rules and to conform to what is labelled normality.

Some Guide and Guardian Spirits

There are different guides and guardians, and listed below are some with whom I have had the privilege of working over the years. There are many more than recorded here.

Angels

The word *angel* is thought to be derived from the Greek word "angelo" which means "messenger." The Christian, Jewish, and Muslim faiths believe that angels act as messengers of God.

Angels are entities made up of light, allowing them to manifest in any form required. They are highly intelligent, have extraordinary strength, and as pure beings of love and light are considered to be extremely holy. Angels are deemed to be the essence of absolute love originating from the heart of the Creator. They come in many forms, but I will focus on two, guardian angels and archangels.

Unlike humans, angels do not have free will, since their sole purpose is to love and serve without condition as the Creator desires. They are very much connected to the godhead and have no spiritual lessons to learn. Some angels, feeling pure love for the earth and its inhabitants, choose to take on physical form to assist at particular stages of evolution. They show the eternal flame of love by their very presence. Many incarnate angels initially find being in a physical body difficult, but all of them at some point will awaken, and their angelic essence will become evident.

All angels are beings of light who respond to our call. They can give great comfort in times of need, and wonderful advice if we are prepared to listen.

If you feel a warm energy, have the sense of wings wrapping themselves about you, or see bright flashes of light like sparkles, then know that an angel is near.

Many people firmly believe that no angel has been or ever will be incarnate, but who is to say what can or cannot transpire? If we keep an open mind and an open heart, we allow ourselves the possibility of experiencing all that the universe has to offer, including meeting an angel in physical form or having otherworldly angelic experiences. Restrictive thinking and belief systems can limit the experience of life as well as supernatural phenomena.

It may be healthier to be an agnostic (a person who does not deny the existence of God but holds that we cannot know for certain whether God exists) rather than an atheist (a person who categorically denies the existence of God) or a person of blind faith (someone who believes without confirmation of God's existence).

Questioning creates opportunities, known or unknown. This in turn enables experience, and it is through our experiences that we create our own truths.

Archangels

The word *arch* means "chief" or "principal." Therefore, *archangel* means "chief angel" or "principal angel." Archangels oversee the other angels including guardian angels. They have the same qualities as angels, but their vibration is much finer, and the heat they emit can be extremely intense. When they connect with you, it is not unusual to find yourself perspiring.

Once you connect with the angelic realm and your ability to sense them heightens, you will be able differentiate between the types of angels. This is most likely to happen through the sensations they give you. For example, when Archangel Michael is acting as a protector, you may see bright blue sparks of light and feel a warm energy surrounding you.

There are many more archangels than those written about by mankind. They are working in the background, and each has a specific task.

It has been said that archangels have never been incarnate, yet the Bible mentions Enoch (the archangel Metatron) and Elijah (the archangel Sandalphon), twin brother of Enoch. Both these men were taken up to heaven as archangels. Apart from our own experience, we cannot confirm whether angels have been or are incarnate. So why not keep an open mind?

Guardian Angel

Our guardian angel's task is to protect, guide, and strengthen us against the forces of negativity. We all have our own guardian angels. They are appointed to us at birth, and will never leave us.

The guardian angel's task is to send us light for inspiration and support, bringing comfort during times of need and assisting us throughout life.

Our first conscious contact with the angelic realm is usually through a guardian angel. The first experience of an angelic presence often comes during times of acute spiritual turmoil, danger, grief, illness, or extreme joy.

Our guardian angel is not allowed to interfere with our free will unless we are in mortal danger and our time to return to spirit would be premature. If we want them to help us, we must give them permission by asking.

When my guardian angel is letting me know he is near, I usually have the sensation of wings sprouting between my shoulder blades. These wings change colour according to the level of danger I am in. When I have been in life-threatening situations, he has on more than one occasion spoken loudly just beside my right ear. His words have been archaic and formal. The most recent intervention came when I was not paying attention while driving. A masculine voice firmly said, "Pay heed!," a term I would never have used. Had he not spoken, I would have continued driving carelessly and would have been hit on the driver's side of the car and would not be writing this today.

Ascended Masters

Ascended masters are individuals who once lived on earth and learned life's lessons during their incarnations. They rose above human restrictions and discovered the meaning of the words "freedom of spirit."

Ascended masters were sources of unconditional love during their lives and by transcending duality (rising above the two sides of ourselves to oneness) became one with their God essences. These highly enlightened beings of the spirit world serve as teachers for mankind. Ascended masters are great teachers because during their lifetimes, they experienced everything that any human can experience. They had to learn the same lessons that we do, and so they can help us grow in any area of our lives. In doing so, they help us to recognise our life purpose and true potential.

Jesus, Buddha, Quan Yin, and many other ascended masters can help us attain the enlightenment that we need to move on to the next phase of our lives.

When I sense ascended masters, I usually feel a gentle stroking on my cheek that lets me know they are present, and I see the number 333 everywhere. Your signs may be different.

Doorkeeper/Gatekeeper

A doorkeeper/gatekeeper defends us, and when asked, will stand at the door or gate between our two worlds. Doorkeepers decide who from the spirit realm to allow near us and are instrumental in checking and managing guides who want to work with us.

Doorkeepers are usually assigned to us when we begin practicing the craft of mediumship, and they work differently from guardian angels and guardian spirits. Their sole purpose is to protect us from the negative elements of the spirit realm, such as beings that are not yet in the light and who intend to cause mischief.

Doorkeepers can be the strong, silent types, and mine very rarely speaks to me, yet I know he is there when I feel the sensation of being clothed in armour. Some people, however, have told me that their doorkeepers are quite chatty, so expect the unexpected.

Guardian Spirit

Along with the guardian angel there is the guardian spirit. These beings are likely to have been warriors in their tribes when incarnate. They are warm and loving and emanate incredible strength and power.

Their presence is very different from that of guardian angels. The guardian spirit, though loving, can produce intense protective vibrations, whereas a guardian angel does not exhibit that human aspect of defence. The guardian spirit's purpose is the everyday security of our spirit and body.

My guardian spirit is a Native American Indian called Wandering Feather. When I have found myself in any nonlife-threatening physical danger, he has quite forcefully stood in front of me.

He is six feet three, has a muscular physique, carries a tomahawk, and is accompanied by an owl and a wolf, which at times appears as a black panther. He was a warrior in his tribe and roamed the lands ensuring that no threat reached his encampment. He has a cheeky sense of humour (very suited to mine), but when there is ill intent around me he is extremely vocal and I have the sense that he grows in stature.

Teacher Guide

Spirit guides of this nature work with us to solve problems. They are assigned to help us complete an experience or life stage. They have a fine vibration and are exceptionally wise.

These guides are at varying stages of their own development, and they come to us when we need help navigating the physical process of life. We may have several of them during a lifetime.

Our level of spiritual awareness and vibration dictates which of these guides our doorkeeper will allow to work with us.

They might come in the form of a healing guide, a lecture guide, a teacher of truth, or any other guide that we might need.

I have worked with the three mentioned above, and I have noticed their common calling card. As they step into my energy field, I feel my neck thicken, which is how I know the being is a teacher guide. If they have feminine energies, they tend to start on the left side of my neck. The masculine energies seem to manipulate my whole neck.

A Simple Guide to Symbols

We often receive communications in our dream state or during meditation. I will refer mostly to what we dream rather than to the state of meditation. However, although symbols tend to be the language of dreams, they can be applied to images received during meditation.

Dream interpretation began around the fourth century BC when people realised that the subconscious mind communicates with us by bringing our deepest concerns and desires to the surface through symbols, usually in the dream state when we are not encumbered by daily issues.

The first step in dream interpretation is to identify the symbols and details we remember from our dreams. Then we must consider what each symbol means to us. We should also determine whether the symbols have anything in common.

The second step is to examine our feelings during the dream. What appeared to be the most important part of the dream? Were we feeling anxious, frightened, sad, happy, or at peace?

The third step is to look beyond the obvious if the obvious has no meaning to us. A physical event in a dream frequently represents mental or emotional matters.

Once we have gained an understanding of a dream, we should consider whether the dream relates to an issue in our life. We must determine if it is linked to a recent event. The most difficult part is identifying the issue. Once that is done, we can understand how it might be resolved.

We must always remember that there are positive and negative sides to everything and that we can use literal or symbolic interpretation. Try the literal approach first, and if that isn't fruitful, examine the information in a symbolic way.

In mediumship work and in meditating, we may feel sensations in different areas of the body. When we experience these sensations, several principles can generally be applied. The left side of the body can be indicative of the past. This side is generally feminine and is classified as assertive or passive. The right side of the body can be indicative of the future. This side is generally male and is classified as aggressive. To remember the difference, keep in mind the phrase "left for ladies," which means that the right side stands only for men and the masculine.

I have listed below some common symbols, most selected from my own experience and others that I have been told about. This list is not comprehensive, and I suggest further research on any symbols not listed here that you may have been encountered.

Credit for most of the descriptions of these symbols goes to Pamela J. Ball, who wrote 10,000 Dreams Explained. I particularly recommend 10,000 Dreams Explained as this book has been instrumental in helping me interpret many things I have dreamt and seen.

Symbols

Angels

Angels seen in a dream symbolise goodness, purity, protection, comfort, and consolation. Pay attention to the messages that the angels are trying to communicate, since these messages serve as a guide to contentment and happiness. On the other hand, they may suggest a disturbance in your psyche.

To dream that you are an angel suggests that you are feeling good about something you said or did. Alternatively, if you have posed the question "Who am I?," the message could be that you are an incarnate angel or that you have angelic qualities.

Three angels seen in a dream are said to symbolise some sort of divinity and are considered a sign of holiness. Seeing an angel holding a scroll indicates high spiritual vision, and your future and your goals may become clearer to you. Pay attention to the message on the scroll, since the contents are normally of particular importance.

Animals

By understanding animals and their symbolism, you can approach life in a simpler, more natural way. Animals are protective and can be teachers. When you need to understand your psychological urges, animals will appear not only in your dreams, but in your daily life. They have symbolic qualities.

When they show friendliness, dogs, cats, and bears offer comfort and protection, horses supply strength, fish provide peace, and birds offer freedom of spirit. Birds such as eagles and hawks also offer protection, and the owl usually represents wisdom.

Snakes seen in a dream can mean that you are dealing with a difficult situation in your waking life. On the positive side, snakes can also mean that healing and transformation are taking place. A spider spinning a web is indicative of your ability to create your reality. Spiders are also a symbol of creativity because of the intricate webs they spin. On a negative note, they may indicate a feeling of being entangled or trapped in a situation.

An animal showing aggression points to your behaviour or that of someone close to you.

Baby

If the baby is your own, this may indicate your need to recognise those feelings of vulnerability over which we have no control. You may be attempting something new.

If the baby is someone else's, you need to be aware of that person's potential to be hurt or of the person's innocence.

The appearance of a baby means that you are in touch with the innocent, curious side of yourself, with the part that neither wants nor needs responsibility. Baby symbolism can indicate that you need to feel purity.

Bells

The bell is an ancient charm against the powers of destruction and is used to clear the atmosphere.

Bells may indicate that you want to communicate with someone who is distant or estranged from you. They may also signify the conscience and the need for approval from others.

A bell, such as a doorbell or ship's bell, warns you to be alert and may point to approaching physical or spiritual danger.

Books

A book, particularly a sacred one such as the Bible or the Qur'an, signifies hidden or sacred knowledge. Any religious book presupposes some kind of spiritual realisation or knowledge gained. It represents our need to delve into the realms of sacred or arcane knowledge or our desire for reassurance that we are going in the right direction.

We are searching for ways to handle what has happened in our lives. Our quest for knowledge and our ability to learn from other people's experiences and opinions are symbolised by books and libraries.

Bottles

The bottle, with its functions of containing and enclosure, is a womb symbol and therefore reflects femininity, fertility, and intuition.

Opening a bottle could mean making available resources you possess but may have suppressed. A broken bottle could indicate aggression or failure. To a certain extent, interpretation depends on which type of bottle is perceived.

When the image is of a baby's feeding bottle, it indicates the need to be nurtured and helped to grow. A bottle of alcohol shows the need to celebrate, or to curb an excess, while a medicine bottle might symbolise the need to examine your health.

Boulders/Rocks

Boulders symbolise obstacles or challenges in life if they are obstructing your way. If this is the case, material embedded in the unconscious may be blocking you in your waking life. When these symbols appear, you might benefit from examining old ideas that no longer serve you.

Candles

Candles have always symbolised illumination, wisdom, strength, and beauty. They now also signify the end of darkness or ignorance.

Lit, they suggest the enduring flame of life and the use of power. Unlit, they indicate potential held in reserve.

Candles can represent knowledge or wisdom that is not yet fully crystallized. Used as tools, they mark our control of personal magic, and dreams will often give information as to their best use.

To dream of candles indicates that you are trying to clarify something that you do not understand. Lighting a candle represents courage and fortitude or a request for something that you need.

Cars/Vehicles

The car represents your personal space, an extension of your being, and relates to the body and its condition.

Always take a note of the colour and condition of the vehicle and the direction in which it is going. Be aware of your health and the conditions of those close to you, since these could be indicated by the condition of the vehicle. Cars also stand for spiritual direction and motivation.

Clocks

The appearance of clocks in a dream is usually indicative of time and could point to the fact that you may not be getting enough rest or may be trying to do too much at once. It is also a reminder to allow time for personal growth. Time also represents change.

Colours

Colour affirms the existence of light. The symbolism of colour in dreams or meditation is significant, since we know that these colours are not physically produced, but are mental images. Here are some meanings given to colours.

Black: This colour suggests negativity, judgement, and the manifestation of mystery.

Blue: A prime healing colour, it suggests relaxation, sleep, and peacefulness.

Brown: The colour of the earth and of commitment, it signifies practicality and grounding.

Green: The colour of nature and plant life, it signifies growth, balance, and harmony.

Gold: This colour indicates a connection with the masculine side of the divine. It also symbolises love and harmony.

Orange: A cheerful and uplifting colour, it has associated qualities of creativity, happiness, independence, health, and vitality.

Pink: A lovely, uplifting colour, it represents love and compassion.

Purple: This colour is indicative of royalty and connection with the higher self.

Red: Life-force energy, vigour, strength, sexuality, and power are all connected with this colour. A beautiful, clear mid-red is the correct shade to signify these qualities.

Turquoise: This greeny blue is taken in some religions to be the colour of the freed soul. It means calmness and purity.

Violet: While found by some to be too strong, this colour means nobility, respect, and hope. Its purpose is to uplift.

White: Containing within it all colours, it suggests innocence, spiritual purity, and wisdom.

Yellow: The colour closest to daylight, it is connected to the emotional self, and its attributes are thought, detachment, and judgement.

Death

Death can signify the end of a relationship, situation, or phase to make way for the new. It may also represent a change of awareness and a shift to the more spiritual self. It does not necessarily stand for death itself. Instead, it can point to the unseen aspects of life, such as omniscience, spiritual rebirth, and renewal.

To dream of your own death suggests that you are exploring your feelings about death, are retreating from the challenge of life, or are investigating your perception of how others feel about you.

You may be becoming conscious of possibilities that you have missed or talents that you have not tapped and feel that you are no longer able to exploit. It is important to be sensitive to your ability to revive these possibilities.

Earth/Earthquake

Earth has many names and is often called Mother Nature, Great Mother, Mother Earth, or Gaia and is therefore synonymous with fertility.

We all have the need to be grounded and practical, but we must have support to be so. If you find yourself under the earth or trapped by it in dreams, you need to be more aware of and understand your unconscious drive and behaviour. Old opinions and attitudes may be fading and relationships may be ending and causing concern.

An earthquake represents spiritual upheaval. When you are conscious of an earthquake, your basic emotional stability will have been called into question.

Dreaming of an earthquake alerts you to an inner insecurity that you must deal with before it overwhelms you. Great inner change and growth are taking place, and they could cause upheaval.

Elements

Since the word *element* means "first principle," spiritually it can point to the Creator. The elements fire, air, water, and earth are deemed to be the first principles of creation. Chinese thought includes metal as the fifth element.

Fire: Fire represents energy and power.

 To be aware of the heat of a fire is to be aware of someone else's strong feelings. Baptism by fire signifies a new awareness, an awakening of spiritual power, and a transformation sometimes created through extreme emotion.

 Fire often appears in dreams as a symbol of cleansing and purification. To be burnt alive may point to our fears of a new relationship or phase in life. We may also be conscious that we could suffer for our beliefs.

Air: Spiritually, air signifies the breath of life.

 Air represents intellect and allows us to bridge the gap between the spiritual and the physical realms. As breath, it is a necessary part of life, but we tend not to think about it until there is a problem.

 Air is a force that supports and surrounds all that we do, so in dreams to be conscious of a bellows or a pump suggests that we need to use strategy and power to achieve our ends.

Water: Water represents spiritual progress and the emotions.

 If the water is clear, then a cleansing, a new beginning, or a washing away of old thoughts and values to make way for new ones is taking place. Muddy or turbulent water reflects the undercurrents in life that must be dealt with.

Earth: Earth signifies stability and grounding. (See "Earth/Earthquakes.")

Metal: The ancients recognised the importance of metal, particularly as an offering to the gods, and much of that symbolism is still relevant today.

 Most metals have symbolic meanings. They can also be connected with planets and other celestial bodies: gold (sun), silver (moon), quicksilver (Mercury), copper (Venus), iron

(Mars), tin (Jupiter), and lead (Saturn). In dreams, these ancient symbols begin to surface as we learn more. For instance, Mars the warrior wielding an iron sword suggests that we need to fight for our interests and become more assertive.

Metals represent the restrictions of the real world. They can be linked with basic abilities and attributes, but also can mean hardness of feeling or emotional rigidity. An article made of lead suggests heavy responsibility.

Family

The family symbolises the spiritual triangle, the unification of love and wisdom from which arises power. It is the group in which we are meant to feel secure.

The struggle for individuality should take place within the safety of the family unit. This does not always happen. In dreams, we can manipulate the images of our family members so that we can work through our difficulties without harming anyone else.

It is also worthwhile to consider the significance of a particular family member or of the relationship we have with that person.

Feathers

Feathers, particularly white ones, are said to symbolise the heavens and messages from the angelic realms and the soul. Spiritual triumph is shown by a display of plumage.

Feathers often represent flight to other parts of the self, and because of their connection with the wind and the air, they can symbolise our more spiritual side. A bird's plumage is its protection, but it is also its power and strength. In this sense, it alerts us to the fact that we can use our own strength and ability to achieve what we want to do.

Feathers in a dream could denote softness and lightness, perhaps the need to take a gentler approach to a situation. We may need to look at the truth of a situation, and recognise that we must behave more calmly.

Plumage can often stand for a display of power and strength. It may also signal defiance, the need to stand firm and show our colours.

Flowers

Flowers signify love and compassion, which we receive and give to others. The feminine principle is often symbolised by flowers. The bud represents potential, while the opening blossom indicates development.

To be given a bouquet means that you are being rewarded for an action. Taking note of the colours is important, since colours have specific meanings.

Researching the meaning of flowers can be beneficial. For example, a daisy can represent wakefulness and awareness.

Food

Food in dreams always symbolises spiritual sustenance, what we need to continue on our journey through life.

Food fulfils certain psychological needs. For example, fruit represents the potential for prosperity if shown as being ripe. The results of our efforts and experiences (the fruits of our labour) may be represented. The colour can also be significant.

Hearts

Your heart seen in a dream signifies truth, courage, love, and romance. It represents how you are dealing with your feelings and expressing your emotions. Depending on how your heart is presented, the message may be that you need to get to the core of a situation before proceeding.

A winged heart represents the power of love and its ability to penetrate through to anyone.

A bleeding or aching heart symbolises desperation, despair, extreme sadness, and sympathy. It means that you lack support or love in some aspect of your life.

Hills or Mountains

Hills and mountains in a dream signify many major obstacles and challenges that must be overcome. To be on top of a hill or a mountain indicates that you have achieved your goals. Mountains also denote a higher realm of consciousness, knowledge, and spiritual truth.

To be climbing a hill or a mountain signifies your determination and ambition.

To fall off a mountain may indicate your rush to succeed without thoroughly considering the path to success. Perhaps you are being pushed upward in a direction that you do not want to go or that you are not ready to take. It could also mean that you have a tendency to give up too easily or flee demanding situations.

House

A house seen in a dream represents your soul and yourself. Specific rooms in the house signify particular aspects of the psyche. In general, the attic equates to your intellect, and the basement depicts the subconscious.

An empty house indicates feelings of insecurity, and a shifting house suggests that you are experiencing personal changes and altering your belief system.

A house without walls represents a lack of privacy. You feel that everyone is looking over your shoulder or interfering in your business.

If you live with others in your waking life, yet dream that you are living alone, this suggests a need to take steps toward independence. You must accept responsibilities and be more self-reliant.

To be locked out of a house represents rejection and insecurity. You feel you are being left behind.

An abandoned house implies that you have left behind your past and are ready to move forward to the future.

An old, run-down house depicts your old beliefs and attitudes and how you used to think or feel. A situation in your life may be triggering those old attitudes and feelings. The old house may also symbolise the need to update your thinking.

A messy and/or dilapidated house implies that an aspect of your life is in chaos. You may be suffering from some emotional or psychological clutter. You need to release these feelings to regain control.

If your house is damaged in the dream, this can indicate your waking concerns about its condition.

To dream of cleaning your house signifies the need to clear out thoughts and get rid of old ways. You are seeking self-improvement.

Seeing a new house indicates that you are entering a new phase or new area in your life. You are becoming more emotionally mature.

If your house has been broken into, this suggests that you are feeling violated. This image may refer to a relationship or situation in your life. It could also indicate that subconscious material is attempting to make itself known. There are some aspects of ourselves that we have denied.

Dreaming that a house has disappeared signifies that you are not feeling grounded. You may feel uprooted by a circumstance or relationship in your life.

To see yourself inside a stranger's house shows that there is something that you have yet to discover about yourself. This could point to memories, fears, or emotions that you are not confronting.

Insects

Insects in a dream signify minor obstacles that you must overcome. Small problems and annoyances must be addressed. You may feel that you are under attack, or something or someone may be bugging you. Alternatively, insects symbolize precision, alertness, and sensitivity. You may need to organise your thoughts and sort out your values.

It is worth noting the type of insect and its colour, since this can be significant. For example, a butterfly represents the freed spirit and immortality. There is no reason to feel trapped by the body, since it can help the spirit grow.

Jewels or Gems

Jewels seen or worn in a dream denote a value within ourselves or within others that we admire and cherish. They also symbolise pleasure, riches, ambition, and spiritual protection.

To find jewels indicates a rapid climb to success. Understanding the use of gems and jewels can greatly enhance personal development. In most dreams, the better-known stones appear. However, when the lesser-known ones are seen, there is much benefit to be gained from learning more about them.

Research each gem, taking note of the colour. For instance, the emerald[3] is a stone of inspiration and infinite patience. It is a life-affirming stone with great integrity. Known as the "stone of successful love," it brings domestic bliss and loyalty. The emerald aids recovery from infectious diseases.

Music

Music expresses ideas and emotions through rhythm, melody, and harmony. Rhythm expresses the essential pulse of life, melody an individual sound, and harmony a pleasing combination of sounds. In dreams, this symbolism reflects man, his concerns, and his society.

Harmonious and soothing music in a dream signifies prosperity and pleasure. You are expressing your emotions in a positive way. Music heals the soul.

Discordant or out-of-tune music indicates unhappiness, lack of harmony, and troubles in a relationship or in domestic life.

Numbers

Numbers drawn to your attention in dreams can have personal or symbolic significance. A number will often have personal meaning;

---

[3]   Judy Hall, *The Crystal Bible: Volume 1: The definitive guide to over 200 crystals.* (Godsfield Press, a division of Octopus Publishing Group Ltd, Great Britain, 2009) (pp 126–127).

it may be a date or the number of a former address. Your mind will often retain significant numbers even though you do not consciously remember them.

As you progress spiritually, you can put the vibratory effect of numbers to good use. It has long been accepted that we can influence our environment by combining numbers in certain ways. Master numbers (eleven, twenty-two, thirty-three, forty-four, fifty-five, and so on) have significant relevance, and researching them would be worthwhile, since from a numerological perspective they can have specific meaning for you.

One: One stands for individuality, autonomy, leadership, originality, confidence, and the sense of self. To be number one means that you are a winner and the best. Alternatively, one signifies solitude or loneliness. It also stands for a higher spiritual force.

Two: Two stands for balance, diversity, partnership, marriage cooperation, the soul, and receptivity. It can also symbolise double weakness or double strength. The world is seen as being made up of dualities and opposites, as in male and female, mother and father, light and dark, heaven and hell, yin and yang.

Three: Three signifies life, vitality, inner strength, completion, imagination, creativity, energy, self-exploration, and experience. Three stands for a trilogy, as in past, present, and future or father, mother, and child, or body, mind, and soul. The number three seen in a dream may be telling us that the third time is the charm.

Four: Four denotes stability, physical limitations, hard labour, and earthly things, as in the four corners of the earth or the four elements (earth, wind, fire, and water). It also stands for material matters and how we get things done. The number four in a dream may be a pun on being "for" a position. In Asian cultures, the number four is a metaphor for death.

Five: Five represents persuasiveness, spontaneity, boldness, a daring nature, action, and humanity. The number represents the five human senses and thus may be telling us to be more sensitive and more in tune with our senses. The number five may also reflect a change in our path or the need to alter our course. It is also the link between heaven and earth.

Six: Six is indicative of cooperation, balance, tranquillity, perfection, warmth, union, marriage, family, and love. It represents harmony in our mental, emotional, and spiritual states. It is also indicative of domestic bliss.

Seven: Seven signifies mental perfection, healing, completion, music, and attainment of high spirituality. The number may also refer to the seven deadly sins, the seven days of the week, or seven chakras. It also indicates uniqueness and eccentricity.

Eight: Eight stands for power, authority, success, karma, material gains, regeneration, and wealth. When the number eight appears in a dream, trust your instincts and intuition. Alternatively, the number may be a pun on *ate*. Perhaps there is information that we need to digest.

Nine: Nine denotes completion, closure, rebirth, inspiration, and reformation. It indicates that we are on a productive path, seeking to improve the world. The number nine also symbolises longevity.

Scissors

Scissors in dreams suggest cutting the nonessential out of our lives. They can also represent a sharp, hurtful tongue or cutting remarks.

Dreaming of sharpening scissors suggests that we need to be more precise in our communication, whereas blunt scissors denote that we are likely to create a problem by speaking too bluntly.

The type of scissors could also be important. Kitchen scissors would, for instance, be more utilitarian than surgical scissors, which would suggest the necessity to be more precise.

Shapes

Geometric shapes that give us a greater understanding of the abstract world may appear in dreams. The number of sides a shape has is significant, as are the colours. Considerable symbology has grown up around shapes. Shapes and patterns can be interpreted.

Circle: The inner being or the self. The circle also means unity and perfection.

Cross: A symbol of spirit made into matter.

Diamond: Indicative of the greater and lesser options available to us.

Hexagon: The geometric figure that makes the most efficient use of space. The cells of the honeycomb are hexagonal for this reason, and this shape epitomises nature's best use of resources.

Oval: Symbolic of the womb, therefore of feminine life. Called the vesica piscis, it is the halo that completely encircles a sacred figure.

Spheres: These indicate perfection and completion of all possibilities.

Spiral: The perfect path to evolution. The principle that everything is continually in motion, but also continually rising or raising its vibration.

Square/Cube: These signify the manifestation of spirit into matter. They represent the earthly realm as opposed to the heavens. The cube is a more tangible representation of this.

Stars: These faraway suns, particularly bright ones, indicate our hopes and ideals. The star represents those things we must reach for.

Swastika: With its arms moving clockwise, it portrays the ideal man and the power he has for good. In Eastern symbolism, the swastika signifies the movement of the sun. A swastika moving anti-clockwise signifies all that is sinister and wrong.

Triangle: A symbol of the standing human with his/her three parts: mind, body, and spirit. Consciousness and love manifest through his/her physicality. There is potential still to be realised.

Shield

In spiritual development, the shield symbolises a particular stage of growth. At this juncture, we need to appreciate that we control our own destiny.

A shield seen in a dream symbolises emotional, spiritual, and physical protection, or we may be feeling vulnerable and in need of comfort.

Spear

The spear signifies directness and honour. It has the power of life and death. The spear is that part of us that is fertile and assertive.

To see a warrior with a spear is to recognise the aggressive male. To put a spear in the ground is to mark one's territory. If you are throwing a spear, you may need to be aware of your assertive tendencies.

Whether it appears in a dream, the spear makes you conscious of the need to cut out nonsense and get straight to the point.

Swimming

To dream that you are swimming suggests that you are exploring aspects of your subconscious mind and emotions. The dream may be a sign that you are seeking emotional support. It is a common dream image for people going through therapy.

To dream that you are swimming underwater suggests that you are completely submerged in your own feelings. You are forcing yourself to deal with your subconscious emotions.

Trees

The tree usually symbolises the basic structure of our inner lives. When a tree appears in a dream, you should try to remember everything about it, since this will tell you a great deal about your inner state of being.

Lush green trees seen in a dream represent new hopes, growth, desires, knowledge, and life. They also imply strength, protection, and stability. You are concentrating on your development and individuation.

A tree with wide branches suggests a warm, loving personality, whereas a small, close-leafed tree suggests an uptight personality. If you cannot identify with either of these types, look to the network of people surrounding you and see if anyone fits the description.

The branches of a tree signify the stages of growth we go through, and leaves suggest the way we communicate with the world. Bare trees suggest used-up energy. You have put your all into a relationship or project and are now exhausted. Perhaps you are feeling depressed. Alternatively, a bare tree signifies the cycle of life or the passage of time.

A withered or dead tree implies that hopes and desires have been dashed. You are experiencing instability and a setback. The dead tree may also represent infertility or a lack of virility. Perhaps it signals an end to a familial line (as in a family tree).

Crows perched on a dead tree symbolise the end of some cycle or behaviour.

Climbing a tree signifies achievement of career goals and attainment of a higher position in life. The speed at which you climb the tree will parallel the speed of your achievement of these goals.

Sitting under a tree alone signifies a time for reflection. You are contemplating an important decision.

Sitting under a tree with someone else suggests that you are evaluating the relationship. The dream may also mean satisfaction with your situation.

To dream that you are chopping down a tree indicates the need for a complete overhaul of your beliefs and ideals and symbolises radical change.

A falling tree means that you are feeling off balance and out of sync. Perhaps you are off track and headed in the wrong direction.

The roots of a tree are said to show our connection with the earth and ourselves. Spreading roots show an ability to relate well to the physical. Deep-rootedness suggests a more self-contained attitude.

The trunk of the tree signifies how we use the energies available to us, and the face that we present to the world. A rough trunk suggests a rough and ready personality, whereas a smoother trunk indicates more sophistication.

Understanding the "Clairs" and Other Gifts

What Are the Different Clairsenses and Other Gifts We Have?

C*lair* is the French word for "clear," so, for example, *clairaudience* means "clear hearing." So what are the clairsenses? This term includes any kind of paranormal feeling related to the five senses of seeing, hearing, smelling, tasting, and touching.

The clairsenses include clairvoyance, clairaudience, clairsentience, clairgustance, and clairtangency. Three other gifts that people can have are channelling, clairempathy, and clairscentience.

In developing spiritual awareness, our extrasensory sensitivity becomes more noticeable, and our receptivity to paranormal phenomena increases. As we become increasingly conscious that our reality is only a fraction of the universal reality of existence, we begin to transcend duality. In doing so, we add senses that extend far beyond those we are accustomed to using. We are then able to use all these and more in our interactions with the spirit world.

Channel and Channelling

A channel is a person who allows his body and mind to be used as an instrument for spirit intelligence to impart healing energy or information to others.

Channelling is the act of allowing ethereal entities to enter the mind and body to impress thoughts upon the consciousness, which are then verbalised or physically delivered by the channel.

Clairaudience

Clairaudience means "clear hearing." This means that our ability to hear extends beyond the physical and moves into the world of the non-material. We are able to hear sounds or words from the universe or realm of spirit, and these come in the form of the "inner ear" or "mental tone," normally inaudible to the physical ear.

Sound is picked up through thought projection. Tones and vibrations are more easily perceived in the alpha mind state and during meditation.

There are two main types of clairaudience, the subjective and the objective. In the subjective version, the sound or vibration is heard internally by the mind. Perhaps repetitive words have entered your mind telling you to call your parents, and when you do, you learn some important piece of news. This is subjective clairaudience.

In the objective version, the sound is heard outwardly. Have you ever heard your name being called, turned to see who was speaking, and found no one there? This is objective clairaudience.

As with any "clair" ability, there may be vast differences in how people experience this. The sound may be perceived as a voice like our own. A thought projection has been received and interpreted through our voice, or it can be experienced as a conversation with another being—for example, hearing someone's voice coming through the mind with the quality and rhythm of his intonation. This usually means that the receiver can identify the speaker's gender and get an instant understanding of the entity, including how the speaker is feeling, by the tone of voice. However, some clairaudients find these voices very different from their own and can hear them inside their heads or right beside an ear. Clairaudience can come in the form of a sensation that words are being poured into the head like a jug of water, and these words may be completely different from the receiver's.

A lot of people experience the first signs of clairaudience when they hear high-pitched buzzing or ringing, wings flapping, ticking, clicking, hissing, or the sound of waves breaking in their ears.

Claircognizance

The word *claircognizance* can be translated as "clear knowing." This communication is not tangible, and generally we have no interest in the subject matter or any idea how we "just know" something. We simply do.

Claircognizance is thought to come directly from the universal consciousness and moves downward through the crown chakra located on the top of the head.

Claircognizant people can easily and immediately access the universal consciousness, retrieving information they need even if they do not realise they are doing so. When the claircognizant have a sense of knowing, they do not need to interpret the material, and usually the bearer of claircognizant information is correct.

This gift is usually used for the benefit of others. Unfortunately, attempting to get instruction for ourselves is often unsuccessful. That is generally the case with this gift.

Clairempathy

The word *clairempathy* means "clear feeling," but it is not the same as clairsentience. Clairempathy is simply "clear empathy." Another person projects a psychological or emotional state toward the empath, which the empath then absorbs. This ability enables the empath to become an emotional or medical surrogate for others and to experience what other people are thinking and feeling.

It is important to understand the distinction between having empathy and being a psychic empath. Empathy is linked with the notion of sympathy and is a normal human characteristic. Most people have an inclination towards empathy, particularly if they were correctly socialised by their parents.

To be a psychic empath is a very different matter. Empaths are highly sensitive not only to the emotions of other people, but to the physical sensations people are experiencing. An empath will take on physical and psychological disorders with the full intensity of the originator. This enables the empath to fully comprehend the level of discomfort another person is suffering. This aspect of their gift is particularly unpleasant for empaths, since it can be extremely distressing and painful. Imagine feeling exactly the same symptoms, including the pain of someone in the full throes of a heart attack! If an empath is unaware of his gift, and therefore has no understanding of what is happening, the force of what he is feeling can also cause considerable psychological distress.

As a result of their ability to absorb the atmosphere around them, empaths tend to experience unexplained mood swings along with the physical symptoms of other people. This can be particularly overwhelming when in crowded places. Based on the emotional imprints left behind, empaths can accurately read objects belonging to other people. They are also wonderful lie detectors and can identify the hidden agendas of others. It is not unusual for an empath to pick up the symptoms, such as an accelerated heart rate, of a person who is being dishonest.

Empaths must develop specific psychic protection techniques and self-care skills to better enable them to manage their gift, and experienced empaths know how to remove residual negativity from their energy auras and replenish their energy.

People and animals are instinctively drawn to psychic empaths, because they are natural healers and their presence alone gives great peace and comfort. They are also excellent advisers because they feel how a person can manage an issue. The one thing common to all empaths is their sense of responsibility to other people. They feel the need to make other people as comfortable as possible in any way they can.

Clairgustance

Clairgustance means "clear tasting." It is the ability to taste a substance without putting anything in the mouth.

Those who possess this gift can perceive the essence of material from the spiritual realms through taste. This is akin to tasting an apple pie when you have not eaten one, because you are reminded of your grandmother's homemade apple pies.

Clairscentience

Clairscentience (also called *clairscent*) means "clear smelling." Those with this gift may smell a fragrance or aroma, for example the smell of fish or the fragrance of a rose, which is not in the immediate environment. These scents are apparent without the help of the nose.

Clairsentience

Clairsentience means "clear feeling" and is the ability to perceive information by sensations received within the body. Clairsentience is often mistaken for clairempathy.

Clairsentients can sense another's feelings, health, and emotional state, giving them greater understanding of a person's state of being. They may briefly absorb what they sense, but they are generally able to clear the sensation very quickly. A clairsentient can feel aspects of living persons or persons in spirit, including their emotional state. Clairsentients can pick up energy vibrations from another and determine whether the person or spirit is of good or bad intention.

The physical sensations that clairsentients feel include pressure or tightness around the head, often described as being like a vise. They may feel tingling, or the sensation that they have nits, at the top of the head. They also experience tingling in the hands, face, or other areas of the body.

How does a clairsentient's gift work? Everything around us, including humans, is made up of energy that rapidly vibrates, and everything has an energy field, also called the aura. Our vibrations enable us to sense the feelings of another person or the connection to a loved one who has passed over to the spirit realm. The finer our vibration, the more intensely we will feel the world around us, including any paranormal activity.

Clairsentience can be a very emotional experience, and because those with this gift can be very in tune with their inner world, their sensitivity to the outer world increases. A sad event could be extremely distressing for a clairsentient, although not quite as bad as it would be for an empath.

Clairtangency

The word *clairtangency* means "clear touching," and this is the "clair" more commonly associated with psychometry.

This gift is usually linked to clairsentience, and the two together allow the person to handle an object or touch an area, then sense through the palms of the hands any information about the article, its owner, or its history not previously known by the clairtangent.

Clairvoyance

Clairvoyance means "clear seeing." This is not sight as we know it, but the ability to connect with another vibrational frequency and see with the mind's eye or the brow/third eye something that exists in another realm.

A clairvoyant receives paranormal impressions and symbols in the form of inner sight or mental images viewed separately from the eyes. These representations are beyond the boundaries of time and space. Generally, these images are more easily seen when we are at rest and our brains have slowed down to the alpha state or during meditation. However, many practicing clairvoyants receive visual information concerning the past, present, and future in a variety of settings.

Some clairvoyants are able, with their eyes open, to see the same images that others perceive through their third eye when their eyes are closed. These people can simultaneously see the spirit realm and the physical environment. They access the gateway between the worlds while fully aware of their surroundings. Unfortunately, this can be quite difficult for clairvoyants, since they often find the domains they are seeing become enmeshed, and they may discover that they can no longer drive vehicles.

Psychometry

A Brief History

J oseph R. Buchanan coined the term *psychometry* in 1842 from the Greek words *psyche*, meaning "soul" or "spirit," and *metron*, meaning "measure."

Buchanan, an American professor of physiology,[4] was one of the first people to experiment with psychometry. Using his students as subjects, he placed medicines in glass bottles, then asked the students to identify each drug only by holding the vial. The success of these experiments proved to be more than just chance, and Buchanan published his findings in the book *Journal of Man*. To explain his observations, he speculated that all objects have "souls" that hold a memory.

William F. Denton, an American professor of geology,[5] was inspired by Buchanan's work. He conducted experiments to see if psychometry would work with his geological samples, and in 1854 he secured the assistance of his sister, Ann Denton Cridge. Denton wrapped his specimens in cloth, ensuring that she could not see them. Taking the wrapped package in her hands, his sister touched it to her forehead and was able to accurately describe the samples through the clear mental images she received.

From 1919 to 1922, Gustave Pagenstecher, a German doctor and physical researcher, identified psychometric abilities in one of his

---

[4] Physiology is the biological study of the functions of living organisms and their parts.

[5] Geology is the scientific study of the origin, history, and structure of the earth.

patients, Maria Reyes de Zierold. He discovered that while holding an object, she could enter into a trance state, enabling her to give details about the object's past and present. Pagenstecher's hypothesis was that a psychometrist could tune in to the experiential vibrations condensed in the object.[6]

What Is Psychometry?

Psychometry is an ability allowing a person to receive impressions of the history of an object by holding it in his or her hands. These impressions can be perceived as images, sounds, smells, tastes, and even emotions. Psychometry is often used in combination with the gift of clairsentience.

Psychometry is a form of "scrying," a term derived from the word *descry,* which means "to catch sight of." It is an intuitive way of seeing something not seen or felt by our normal senses. Scrying is often done using a crystal ball, black-backed glass, or a bowl of clear water. However, the "sight" in psychometry comes through touch.

For example, a psychometrist can hold an antique watch and relate information about its history, the person who owned it, and the experiences that person had whilst in possession of the watch. The psychometrist may be able to sense the owner's personality, what he did, and even how he passed away. It is not unusual for a psychometrist to feel the emotions of the owner of the object at a particular time, since it would appear that our feelings are most strongly imprinted into our belongings.

---

[6] About.com. 2006. "What You Need to Know About Psychometry" by Stephen Wagner. Access date: August 2012. http://paranormal.about.com/cs/espinformation/a/aa063003.html:

Can I Develop the Gift of Psychometry?

Yes, and in developing this aspect of your talents, you will often find your clairsentience gift beginning to surface. Here is an exercise you can try with the help of a friend.

1. Sit in a quiet location with your phone turned off.
2. Close your eyes, relax, and put your hands on your lap, palms facing up. Allow yourself to be open to receiving images or feelings from whatever object you will be holding. Focus your attention on all the sensations you begin to receive in and on your body, thereby raising your level of awareness.
3. Keeping your eyes closed, ask someone to put an object in your hand. If there is more than one person with you, the person who places the item should be silent so you do not know who did it. The object ideally will be something that has been with that person for a long time, and you will know nothing about it.
4. Stay relaxed and speak out loud any pictures, feelings, words and impressions that come to you.
5. Even if it does not make sense to you, mention everything you pick up, without editing or analysing the information. The material might be relevant to the owner of the object you are holding.

It takes practice to become proficient in the art of psychometry. Once you become more experienced, you can "download" information more easily.

The most experienced psychometrists have an accuracy rate of 70 to 80 percent, so do not give yourself a hard time if you do not achieve 100 percent accuracy. Have fun with this exercise!

AURAS

What Is the Aura?

English Dictionary[7] defines the aura as "a particular quality or atmosphere surrounding a person or thing."

The aura is an electromagnetic field that surrounds the human body. This human energy field is made up of electromagnetic energies[8] that vibrate at different velocities. These energies filter through our energy centres (chakras), drawing in vital life-giving force or expelling harmful energy that we may have absorbed from our environment.

The aura consists of seven layers of subtle energy bodies[9] that exist around the body, and each level pulsates at its own frequency. These layers are interconnected, affecting one another and influencing a person's thoughts, emotions, and behaviour, thereby determining the individual's health and well-being.

Everything we think, do, or feel has an effect on our aura. Thus it is in a constant state of flux based on our mental and physical health. It is also affected by the energies in our environment that permeate all forms

---

[7]   English Dictionary (Gedes & Grosset, an imprint of Children's Leisure Products Limited, Scotland, 1999) pp 36

[8]   Electromagnetic energy is energy from a magnetic field that is produced by the motion of electric charges, such as electric current

[9]   An energy body is electromagnetic energy that vibrates at its own frequency

of matter. The aura is our electronic signature, and a state of imbalance in one energy body will result in instability in the others.

The human aura is at times called a magnetic force field because it has attracting and repelling properties similar to those of a magnet. However, the human aura is far more complex and varied than the simple north and south poles of a magnet. Nevertheless, the following analogy may help in understanding how the aura functions.

A magnet has an energy field around it that pulls objects containing iron towards it. The power of this energy field is discerned when attempting to separate two magnets that have been attracted to each other. The repelling action can be felt as a magnet pushes away another magnet with the same pole, and no amount of pushing can force them together.

Quantum physicists have confirmed what mystics and ancient civilizations have always known: that everything in the universe vibrates with energy. These scientists have accepted that we are more than just our physical bodies and that everything, including human beings and our thoughts and consciousness, is perpetually pulsating with energy at varying densities.

Auras around living (animate) objects, such as people and plants, change moment by moment. However, the aura around nonliving (inanimate) objects such as stones and water is basically changeless, although it can be manipulated by our conscious intent.

What Are the Seven Layers of the Aura?

Each energy body (layer) of our aura relates to one level of our seven core chakras, ranging from the densest (etheric body), which correlates to our base/root chakra, to the finest (ketheric body), which is connected to the crown chakra.

They all have functions that serve the body by drawing in all aspects of life force that we require for survival.

1. Etheric Body (First Layer)

This layer extends a quarter inch to two inches (0.625–5 cm) from the body and is linked to the base/root chakra. It is closest to the line of the body and is consistent in size. The etheric body relates to the physical well-being of the human structure.

This energy body is the most easily seen, and the colours noted in it vary from white to light blue to grey.

2. Emotional Body (Second Layer)

This level is more fluid than the first layer and extends around one to three inches (2.5-7.5 cm) from the body. The second layer is associated with our emotions and corresponds to the sacral chakra.

The hues emitted by the emotional body vary in radiance and tend to be the colours of the rainbow. If a person is discontented, the colour may be a little dirty in appearance.

3. Mental Body (Third Layer)

The mental body extends three to eight inches (7.5-20 cm) from the body and is connected with the solar plexus chakra. The third layer lies beyond the emotional body and is associated with psychological thought processes, ideas, and core values.

When healthy, this layer is composed of clear yellow, green, or blue colours.

4. Astral Body (Fourth Layer)

The astral body (sometimes called the causal body) lies beyond the mental body, and extends six to twelve inches (15-30 cm) from the human form. It is linked to the heart chakra and is associated with our ability to love without condition.

This fourth layer is composed of "clouds" of colour, and the shades generally do not vary. However, they are often infused with light pastel pink.

When the astral body is healthy, colours are vibrant and we find unconditional love effortless. Altruism becomes a natural part of our lives with no expectations of return.

5. Etheric Template (Fifth Layer)

The etheric template lies beyond the fourth layer and extends twelve to twenty-four inches (30-60 cm) from the body. It is linked with the throat chakra and is connected with all forms of communication. This is the level where our higher selves can communicate with the spiritual plane, connecting us to the higher purpose of manifesting our future potential.

The colour usually observed here is blue-grey. Poor health or blockages can be discovered and treated within the etheric body, which sends the information to the physical body.

6. Celestial Body (Sixth Layer)

This layer (sometimes called the intuitive body) lies beyond the etheric template and extends twenty-four to thirty-five inches (60-87.5 cm) from the body. It is linked with the brow/third eye chakra and is associated with intuitive knowledge and spiritual awareness. This is the area where all memories of our connection with the universal one consciousness are stored.

The celestial body is where we connect emotionally when we are experiencing spiritual ecstasy. Its colour is likened to mother of pearl.

7. Ketheric Body (Seventh Layer)

The ketheric body (sometimes called the causal template body) lies beyond the celestial body and extends thirty-five to forty-six inches (60-115 cm) from the body. It is linked with the crown chakra.

This seventh layer connects us to all knowledge held in the universe. It is the link to our inner divine selves, and imprints of our experiences during various incarnations are preserved here.

The ketheric body is frequently filled with iridescent light surrounded by a halo of gold or silver, which serves as an outer border of protection holding all the other layers together.

The Seven Layers of the Human Aura

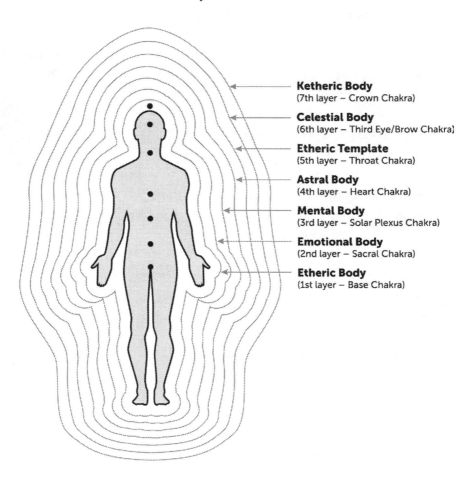

Ketheric Body
(7th layer ~ Crown Chakra)

Celestial Body
(6th layer ~ Third Eye/Brow Chakra)

Etheric Template
(5th layer ~ Throat Chakra)

Astral Body
(4th layer ~ Heart Chakra)

Mental Body
(3rd layer ~ Solar Plexus Chakra)

Emotional Body
(2nd layer ~ Sacral Chakra)

Etheric Body
(1st layer ~ Base Chakra)

How to Sense and See the Human Aura

The majority of people must train themselves to detect the aura, but it is a much easier process than you might imagine.

I will offer the method I use to feel and see auras. However, use whichever technique works best for you if you find that my method is unsuccessful.

Sensing Your Aura

The best way of sensing your aura is by using your hands. The following exercise produces encouraging results.

1. Ensure that you are sitting comfortably and will not be disturbed by external noises.
2. Hold your palms close together without letting them touch. Slowly separate your hands, then bring them back together again. It may take a few attempts before you feel anything. Moving your palms backward and forward, you will feel the energy. Keep doing this until you are comfortable that you are feeling something. Take note of how the energy between your hands feels.
3. As you move your hands back and forth, you will notice a sensation building up in your palms. It may feel tingly or hot, and the increasing energy between your hands will become more evident. It will feel bouncy and light, and you will notice a slight resistance forming between your hands.
4. Keep moving your hands backward and forward, slowly increasing the space between them until you are unable to feel any resistance. You will sense that you have lost the connection. This will give you a good idea of how far your aura extends from your palms.

Now that you have felt your aura, perhaps you want to know which of your hands is the more sensitive. This exercise is one I used to discover which of my hands was not only the more sensitive to auras, but which was the receiver of energy. The other proved to be the sender.

1. Do exercises one to three above to raise your sensitivity to your aura.

2. With your left hand raised above your right forearm, slowly move your hands from your elbow to the tips of your fingers and back again. Take note of how the energy feels in your hand and how much you feel in your forearm. Is the energy that you are receiving in your arm warm, or is it cool like wind blowing? Does the energy feel pleasant and comfortable?

   Now do the same with your right hand over your left forearm.

3. Whichever hand felt the most natural is usually the sender. I feel a warm and sometimes quite hot energy pulsating from my right palm. The area over my body that I am feeling will immediately warm up and become relaxed. My receiver hand still feels somewhat warm, but the energy emitted is subtler.

As a result of using these exercises, I can place my right hand into a person's aura and scan him for hot or cold spots. What I find is usually indicative of the person's emotional state or physical discomfort.

Seeing Your Aura

This exercise takes practice, but you might immediately see something. The more you do it, the easier it will be for you to see the colours emanating from your body.

Seeing your aura for the first time is very exciting. In your excitement, you may focus on the area where you saw the colours. It will immediately disappear. This is perfectly normal, and when you refocus you will be able to see it again. The key is to keep staring at one spot without getting distracted.

1. Stand in front of a mirror about a foot away with your legs spread about a shoulder width apart. Let your arms hang loosely by your sides. Ensure that you have a plain, pale wall behind you and that the light in the room is bright but not dazzling.

2. Look at the space just above your head and relax your eyes. (Allowing your eyes to go slightly crossed will help them to relax. Remember to uncross them!)
3. Keep looking above your head. It may take a while, but you will see a hazy grey or white outline around your head. This may change to a shade of blue. This layer is the etheric body.
4. If you find that staring at the top of your head produces no results, look at the area just beside one of your ears. You may find that you begin to see a shape forming around that side of your body. You have just seen your aura!

What Do the Colours in My Aura Mean?

Our lifestyles and environment affect our auras, and the colours emitted reflect the health of our mind, body, and spirit. The human aura reveals information about our characters and how we are handling situations. The aura is also a bit like an early warning system for illness, offering signs long before the onset of symptoms.

The aura is extremely fluid, and the colours within it vary from moment to moment, reflecting our changing emotions, thoughts, and behaviours.

Colours Commonly Seen in the Aura

The following colours are commonly seen in the aura, although many more variations can be found.

Red

Reds are usually indicative of personality, vitality, power, success, sexuality, strength, courage, action, and survival instincts. Reds are associated with the base/root chakra.

Positive Qualities: When the colour is a vibrant and bright one such as scarlet, the person has health along with passion, self-confidence, and a sense of security. Vibrant reds are usually seen in people who are said to have great charisma and/or sex appeal.

Negative Qualities: A muddy red could indicate a feeling that the life force is being drained. If the colour is a harsh red, it could signify impulsiveness, irritability, or high blood pressure.

Orange

Oranges tend to show creativity, fertility, stimulation, confidence, the ability to relate to others, sociability, intuition (gut feelings), a sense of self-identity, and vitality. This colour is associated with the sacral chakra.

Positive Qualities: When the orange is bright and rich, it denotes the free flow of creative juices and an enthusiastic, optimistic personality disposed toward open-mindedness. Bright oranges indicate a normal metabolism, an efficient immune system, a regular pulse rate, and healthy reproductive organs.

Negative Qualities: When the colour is dull or murky, it could indicate disharmony in a person's life. A pale orange can point to low self-esteem and loss of a sense of self. Should the colour be harsh, then the person may be a little eccentric. Cloudy orange may indicate allergies, infections in the reproductive system, and menstrual pain.

Yellow

Yellow denotes the intellect and new ideas. It is the colour of the thinker. Yellow also signifies inner joy, including the ability to laugh and have fun. This colour is associated with the solar plexus chakra.

Positive Qualities: When the yellow is vibrant and healthy, the mind may be focussed on science, planning, new ideas, or creating knowledge. This yellow is indicative of a good memory and excellent powers of concentration. A brilliant yellow could reveal a person gifted in the performing arts. It shows that a person has healthy lymphatic, nervous, and digestive systems.

Negative Qualities: A murky yellow points to hyperactivity, and mustard yellow could be indicative of jealousy and resentment. Metallic, hazy yellow reveals that an individual may not be honest or is acting with ill intent. It may indicate that a person is suffering from tension, stress, or nervous exhaustion.

Green

Green is the colour of harmony and balance, and is linked with the earth, and therefore nature and the environment. It is associated with the heart chakra.

Positive Qualities: When it is a rich, beautiful emerald, green reveals that an individual is a generous, loving soul who is likely to be a naturally gifted healer and who is loyal, honest, and always speaks from the heart with the best of intentions. It is not uncommon to find emerald green in the halo seen around the heads of healers, particularly those following a life path in the healing field. A clear green could indicate stable blood pressure and a healthy heart and respiratory system.

Negative Qualities: If the green is cloudy or dull, it could indicate that a person has conflicting emotions and may be vulnerable to infections. Yellow present in the green could be a sign of possessive jealousy. Lime green can indicate stress within relationships. Metallic green could point to food allergies and panic attacks.

Blue

Blue is the colour of spiritual truths. All people have some form of blue in their auras. This colour is linked to ideals and the expansion of spiritual and physical possibilities. Blue is associated with the throat and brow chakras; a sky blue relates to the throat chakra, and darker blues tend to correlate with the brow/third eye chakra.

Positive Qualities: When the blue is rich in colour, it can indicate that a person has found the right path in life and is comfortable with leadership. A person with this colour has a keen sense of justice and is inclined to weigh facts before acting or speaking. Pale blue can indicate an idealist who wants to make the world a better place. A bright blue indicates that an individual will put values before personal gain. Clear blue is a sign of stable blood pressure, a regular heart rate, and hormonal balance.

Negative Qualities: A dull blue can indicate an extremely conservative individual. Harsh blue can signify a person with control issues, someone who likes to be in charge of everything. A dull blue can point to depression and throat or teeth problems. An overactive thyroid can show up as a murky blue. A harsh metallic blue can indicate an individual who suffers with migraines and headaches.

Indigo

Indigo indicates spiritual awareness, independence, fearlessness, sensitivity, and compassion. This colour in the aura reveals a person who is seeking spiritual truths. Indigo is associated with the brow/third eye chakra.

Positive Qualities: Indigo seen in the aura denotes a high level of awareness, honesty, and loyalty.

Negative Qualities: Indigo could indicate that a person feels like an outsider, usually because his individualism is often misunderstood.

Violet

Violet in the aura indicates a charismatically powerful and dynamic person who is a great visionary. Violet is linked to the crown chakra.

Positive Qualities: The violet aura reveals an individual who wants all humanity to live in perfect harmony. This is also the colour of a master teacher. The person can be a great inspirational motivator, leading by example. Violet appears when the person has committed himself to spirituality and/or to humanitarian work.

Negative Qualities: Too much violet in the aura can show that a person daydreams too much and has his head in the clouds, which can prevent him from following his true path.

Purple

Purple in the aura indicates spiritual enlightenment and inner vision. This colour is linked to the brow/third eye and crown chakras.

Positive Qualities: A rich shade of purple reveals a person who is connected to his inner wisdom and the collective one consciousness. A clear colour denotes awareness and natural intuitive abilities. A rich, clear purple suggests that the mind, body, and spirit are working in harmony.

Negative Qualities: A blurred purple can show that a person spends too much time in the world of fantasy. A dark purple may reveal someone who feels alone. A dull, cloudy purple could point to infections of the ears and/or eyes, headaches, nightmares, or insomnia.

Turquoise

This is the colour for integration of mind and heart, feelings and thoughts, and wisdom and experience, and it is associated with the heart and throat chakras.

Positive Qualities: A bright, rich turquoise can indicate a poet, inventor, or artist. Those with this colour in their auras are naturally protective of others and readily defend the weak. This colour is associated with stimulation and strengthening of the immune system. Turquoise soothes inflammation, calms nerves, and aids healing.

Negative Qualities: This colour has no negative aspects.

Pink

Pink in the aura represents unconditional love, compassion, and kindness. It is associated with the heart chakra.

Positive Qualities: A clear pink can indicate a person is a natural mediator and friend to the vulnerable. A vibrant pink reveals balanced emotions, regular sleep patterns, and the ability to preserve relaxation. A person with clear pink in his aura can heal children and animals, which are naturally drawn to this individual's loving energy.

Negative Qualities: A harsh pink may suggest occasional over-possessiveness towards family and children. The person is predisposed to get headaches or earaches. A transparent pink may point to physical and emotional exhaustion. Coral pink is a sign of unreciprocated love.

White

White in the aura indicates a person in perfect balance and harmony. This colour is associated with the crown chakra.

Positive Qualities: Brilliant white signifies a highly evolved and enlightened being. The individual has connected with his inner divinity and has a sense of wholeness.

Negative Qualities: A pale white can suggest that a person is out of touch with the real world, while a murky white may point to feelings of alienation.

Grey

Grey appearing in the aura reveals that a person is a keeper of secrets. This is the colour of adaptability and compromise. It is linked to the base/root chakra.

Positive Qualities: A silver-dove grey can indicate that a person is a mediator, someone who is able to remain impartial in difficult situations and resist stress.

Negative Qualities: A dull grey suggests depression. A pale grey can be a sign of unwillingness to confront issues or of indecisiveness. It can also point to an exhausted temper that has left the immune system less effective than usual.

Brown

Brown in the aura denotes a nurturer who accepts his own shortcomings and those of others. Such people are generally very earthy and well grounded. This colour is connected to the base/root chakra.

Positive Qualities: A rich golden brown can indicate an individual who loves nature and Mother Earth. The person has reserves of life-force energy and physical strength. A warm brown reveals a nurturer, and deep brown denotes an intuitive wisdom.

Negative Qualities: Murky brown can point to extravagance and blinkered viewpoints. A harsh brown can reveal that a person is obsessed with money and material gain, no matter what the cost. A dull shade can show overwork, stress, or blockages in the other chakras.

Black

Black in the aura is indicative of change and transformation, including an acceptance of life as it is. This colour is associated with the base/root chakra.

Positive Qualities: A clear, almost transparent black can show a person who is resting emotionally and spiritually.

Negative Qualities: A matt black can suggest depression or exhaustion. A harsh black can reveal a person who frequently offloads problems onto other people, ignoring any feedback. Black spots may point to some part of the body that is unbalanced or indicate that energy is not flowing freely. A person could be harbouring negative behaviour patterns requiring attention.

Silver

Silver in the aura indicates a person who is undergoing steady growth, has intuitive wisdom, and is connected to the divine feminine element within. This colour is associated with the brow/third eye chakra.

Positive Qualities: Silver stars or streaks show hidden potential that will bring joy. This colour can be a sign of pregnancy or a time when conception is possible. It can also denote that the seeds of creativity are being sown and that the imagination is awakening. Silver can reveal that the individual is rediscovering his or her libido.

Negative Qualities: Metallic silver can signify that a person craves excitement and stimulation and thus wants to appear alluring and mysterious. Matt silver can be a sign of fluid retention and the inability to progress emotionally and psychologically.

Gold

Gold in the aura shows a person who is connected to the divine masculine element within. The individual is a visionary whose life will affect others positively. This colour is linked to the crown chakra.

Positive Qualities: A bright, healthy gold indicates divine protection, long life, and plenty of vitality. The individual has a natural regenerative capacity for body and mind.

Negative Qualities: Harsh gold can indicate a desire for wealth and an obsession with power, often at the cost of other people. A tarnished gold may suggest a tendency towards addictions, compulsions, and obsessions.

Placement of Colours in the Aura

The location of colours in the aura provides additional information about what is happening with the individual.

Placement of colours on the left and right sides of the body is not what a medium feels when giving a reading.

During a reading, energy felt by the medium on the left side of the body normally indicates past events and the feminine, passive aspect that must be conveyed to the sitter. The right side is indicative of future events and the masculine, aggressive aspect.

Placement of colours in the aura on these sides of the body has no bearing on a reading given by a medium.

Above the Head

The colour over the head is what we experience in the present moment. It reflects what we think or believe and shows our state of mind.

Left Side of the Body

The left side is indicative of the future. The colour is generally the vibration coming into being. It is what we feel inside but may not have expressed. The closer it is to us, the sooner it will be felt. This could take anywhere from moments to months.

Right Side of the Body

The right side is generally indicative of the energy being expressed in the present moment. This is the vibration frequency most likely seen or felt by others around us. It is the energy we are putting out to the world.

How We Relate to Others Through Energy

Have you ever walked into a room and known that an argument has just taken place even if the room was recently vacated? Have you ever met someone and for no apparent reason taken an immediate dislike to him? Or have you instantly been drawn to someone? Understanding these feelings and reactions can be easier when we learn how we relate to other people through our energy.

The aura is composed of constantly vibrating energy. This energy changes according to our emotional, psychological, and physical states. Due to its fluidity, your aura will connect with the auras of other people, and depending on the relationships you have with these people, your aura may blend with or repel theirs. The ideal relationship will have the energies of people merging harmoniously, easily disconnecting when they physically separate.

In a destructive co-dependent relationship, the auras of two people may have blended to such a degree that they have become almost a single energy field. Disconnection on emotional and physical levels becomes much more difficult and in some cases may be extremely distressful.

On the other hand, someone with a strong, clear aura will positively affect those around him, bringing calm, pleasure, and emotional contentment.

How Our Aura Attracts Others by Our Intention

Our energy will flow where we direct it. This belief has been held by many cultures for hundreds of years. It is confirmed by the knowledge that we are more likely to achieve our goals once we have identified what they are and have turned our attention to reaching them.

If we hold the intention of doing what is best for others, we will attract those who wish the best for us. Likewise, if our focus is on the manipulation of others, we are likely to experience manipulation by others.

Through the ages, this belief system has produced many adages, such as "What goes around comes around" and "He who lives by the sword dies by the sword."

Strengthening and Refreshing the Aura

I have used the following six ways to strengthen and cleanse my aura and have found all of them to be extremely effective.

Black Tourmaline Crystal

Black tourmaline is great for repelling radiation and is known for transmuting harmful energy from the aura. This protective stone can also help combat negative thinking and is wonderful to have close to the body or in your bag or pocket.

Many crystals can help in protecting and rebalancing the aura. I recommend doing research to find the ones that resonate with you. I found that turquoise, lapis lazuli, and amethyst work very well, and I use them in conjunction with black tourmaline. You can find crystals at any metaphysical store.

Feather Aura Clearing

Turkey feathers are very good for cleansing the aura. Take a feather in your dominant hand and gently stroke your aura, keeping the feather about twenty centimeters from your body. Start from your head and work your way down to your feet. If you are unable to reach your back, ask someone to do it for you. Afterwards you should find that your aura feels lighter.

Sage Smudge Stick

The smoke from white sage is known by Native American Indians to be cleansing and purifying. White sage has been used with great success for many years to remove negative energy.

To cleanse your aura, light your sage smudge stick and use your hand or a feather to direct the smoke over your entire body. Using a feather helps waft the smoke over your back.

Sea Salt

Swimming in the ocean or soaking in a salt-water bath helps cleanse the aura, drawing out negativity. The sun expands and revitalises your aura whilst the sea carries away stresses.

If there is no bath in your home and you are not near the ocean, simply give your body a sea-salt scrub before taking a shower. Take a handful of sea salt and rub it all over your skin (avoiding your face and the delicate areas around your eyes) before showering. This assists in getting rid of dead skin, draws out toxins, and refreshes your aura.

Sound Vibration

Sound has been acknowledged by many cultures as a healing modality. Tibetan singing bowls and crystal bowls are well known for their ability to dispel negativity and clean the energy bodies of the aura with the sound they emit.

Alternatively, chanting the om sound is a fast and efficient way to shift stagnant negative energy from the aura and the body.

Sunshine Aura Cleansing

Sunshine is known to nourish and expand the aura. Spending time outside amongst nature makes your mind, body, and spirit feel wonderful and is a natural cleanser. Do it sensibly, though. Twenty minutes in moderate sunshine will make you feel revitalised and happy, which means your aura has been thoroughly cleansed.

DIFFERENCES BETWEEN MEDIUMS AND PSYCHICS

What Is a Medium?

A medium is a person who can communicate with the spirits of those who have passed away. This is usually done by tuning in to the frequency emitted by the spirit entity. The medium then acts as a channel between the worlds of the living and the dead and will interpret any messages given by those in spirit. This means the "reader" (the medium) will inform the "sitter" (the living person to whom the medium is relaying messages) of any details or signals from the spirit world.

Mediums usually have an array of abilities at their disposal, but the purpose behind these gifts is to prove the existence of life after death, to console and to advise others, and to increase their own spiritual enlightenment.

They very rarely use tools of the trade such as tarot cards or runes during a sitting unless they are combining the reading with a psychic interpretation to predict future events.

However, it is my experience that a medium generally will not make predictions, since free will permits people to change their destiny and therefore any prophecies.

A medium will generally give the sitter several pieces of information:

1. Who the communicating spirit is. Mediums may provide a name and a physical description. They are likely to detail any distinguishing

features of the presenting spirit and note the clothes and/or jewellery being worn. A reader will establish the relationship between the communicator and the sitter such as mother, father, grandmother, grandfather, aunt, uncle, or friend, and inform the sitter of any additional presenting entities.

2. Evidence that the spirit entity is who the medium says it is. Readers may describe how the spirit passed over, the illness the person suffered, and the person's occupation, habits, and hobbies. Mediums may recount an event that the sitter will recall, or describe pets (living or passed over) that the sitter might remember. Spirits might speak of special occasions that are coming up and may identify themselves by allowing the medium to detect certain scents that the sitter will recognise, such as perfume, tobacco, or flowers. My grandmother always sends wafts of a perfume called Opium (her favourite but one she knows I detest!).

3. The purpose of the communication, which may include descriptions of past and present conditions in the sitter's life. Mediums may also disclose future events, although only if deemed necessary.

What Is a Psychic?

A psychic is a person who is sensitive to the electromagnetic energies emanating from auras. Psychics can access information from the emotional, physical, and spiritual parts of the auric field. Thus psychic readings can be very accurate, since the aura contains all the information about a person's life.

Psychics tend to work at an intuitive level through a sixth sense or extrasensory perception and generally use the gift of clairsentience to scan the aura and provide insights in many areas such as love, money, career, or travel. However, they often use a variety of tools, such as tarot cards or crystal balls, to assist with predicting future events.

A psychic directly interacts with the sitter and is not generally able to contact spirits.

Fake psychics will not be able to read a person's aura. They use extraordinary powers of observation of nonverbal communication, such as body language, facial expressions, clothes, and jewellery, to conduct a reading. These people are working with ill intent and are master manipulators.

What Is the Difference Between Mediums and Psychics?

The majority of people think that a psychic is also a medium. However, these two terms are totally different. All mediums have psychic abilities, but generally a psychic is not a medium. A person with both of these gifts is often called a psychic medium.

True mediumship abilities are usually untaught and tend to be an inherent part of a person (even if he or she does not understand the gift). Conversely, psychic abilities can be learned by everyone who wishes to develop this skill.

It is important to understand the abilities of mediums and psychics to get a reading that provides the insight you seek.

Can I Develop Mediumship Skills?

Yes, you can, although it may take a little longer to develop these skills than it would for a person who has been able to communicate with the spirit world since childhood.

First, you need to determine the level of your abilities by evaluating your spiritual senses, known as the clairsenses. Refer back to the section "Understanding the "Clairs" and Other Gifts" to recap what they are. Most people, when in tune with their bodies, will find that one of the "clairs" is their predominant sense, and it is usually coupled with a secondary clairsense. However, some people can access a number of clairsenses to give a reading.

Learn to Ground and Clear Your Energy Field

The best way to ground your energy is through meditation, which should always be done before any spirit world communication. It is important to become quiet, close your eyes, and imagine tree roots coming from your feet. Imagine them reaching deep within Mother Earth and firmly rooting you in place. After any reading for which you have grounded yourself, you will need to return the roots from the earth to your body. Do this by imagining them detaching from Mother Earth and moving back into your feet.

Once you have done this, you will need to clear your energy, and the easiest way to do this is to sit quietly, close your eyes, and imagine white light surrounding you. Then visualise or sense the light beginning to dissolve all negative and unwanted energies until only white light remains.

Once you have become familiar and proficient with your intuitive senses, including grounding and clearing your energy, you will have developed the necessary tools to communicate with those in the spirit realm. However, be aware that conversing with discarnate entities takes practice and may not happen immediately.

Which of the Clairsenses is My Predominant Gift?

The exercise below is a good way to identify which of your senses you use the most when communicating with the spirit world.

1. To assess your abilities, shuffle a deck of regular playing cards, then pick up the top card. Before turning it over, ask yourself if it is red or black. Try not to guess, since the point of this exercise is to see how the answer comes to you. Did you hear it in your head? Did you see it as an image when you closed your eyes? Did you sense it was a certain colour? Did you get a physical signal when you said the colour to yourself? Perhaps you received a tingle or energy rush throughout your body.

2. Once you have clearly established the answer, say it out loud and then turn the card over. Did you correctly identify the colour?

   If you were not correct, there could be two reasons your answer was wrong. First, impatience got the better of you and you decided to guess, since you didn't feel anything was coming to you. Second, you may have heard, seen, or sensed the answer, but self-doubt led you to think that you made it up. In doing so, you dismissed the answer you were given, believing that it could not be accurate.

The adage "Practice makes perfect" is noteworthy. As with any developing skill, it's important to keep practicing. In time, you will have a clearer understanding of how you receive intuitive information.

Sensing Spirit

These steps are ways to become competent in your abilities. However, once you are proficient, you would benefit from becoming part of a group that gathers together at least once a week to relay messages from the universe or spirit realm.

The instructor of a group should always protect the meeting place by summoning a dome of white light prior to a group sitting. A group will usually have a doorkeeper/gatekeeper (see "Guide and Guardian Spirits") who ensures that only beings of light may enter the gathering place. The doorkeepers of group members will often attend to defend those under their guardianship from unwanted negative energies.

Once you have grounded your energy, mentally ask who is there. Wait for an answer. When you see an image, get a feeling, hear a name, or receive information from any other sense, calmly state that you have something. Verbalise what you have been given, and someone in the group may confirm the message.

At first, you may not get a great deal, but over time you will receive more, so focus on what you get and trust that it is correct.

It is important to realise that even practicing mediums are human and are therefore rarely 100 percent accurate. Neither is science, which is based on theory until someone comes up with something concrete. Therefore learn to believe in the abilities you possess.

State the Message

State the message you are receiving such as "I have a father figure here who says he was a chain smoker." A member of the group may recognise the person. Once you have confirmation, ask the spirit for his or her name, how he or she died, what his or her occupation was, and for any shared memories this person had with the sitter. When answers are received, say them out loud and allow the person to confirm the messages.

Mediums should ask only for yes-or-no answers from sitters. Occasionally they may explain things, but if you are a medium, it is your duty to produce relevant information.

Remember to thank your spirit guides and guardians for their assistance after any reading or message giving. They appreciate it the same way we do when someone says thank you.

Responsibilities of Mediums and Psychics

Each person has different ways of communicating with those in spirit. Clairaudience may be the primary gift of some, whilst others might be particularly clairvoyant or clairsentient. Our gifts are unique, and no two mediums or psychics are the same.

The methods I have mentioned are helpful ways to sharpen your abilities, and after practicing and gaining confidence in giving readings within the security of a group, you may feel that you are ready to read one on one for others. However, remember that you will be in a position to affect another person's life, and therefore you have a moral duty to behave with integrity.

Keep two points in mind if you decide to use your gifts to read for others. First, ensure that the sitter has given consent, and second, make sure that your intentions are pure when giving a reading.

Honest psychics and mediums would rather tell a sitter that they are getting nothing than to pluck things out of thin air. All mediums have off days when they find it difficult to tune in to the frequencies being emitted. A reader may, for example, be recovering from an illness. However, even on a bad day a medium will get a lot of the information correct, which is how you can identify frauds.

There are people who use their gifts with ill intent, be it for personal gain or to manipulate others. As a psychic medium, I have over the years come across those who have attempted to manipulate me when giving me a reading. I have been appalled by their blatant abuse and greed. Usually their unscrupulous behaviour becomes obvious when they are challenged and turn hostile. Confrontations generally ensue when I find that information given about my past or present is completely wrong. This normally tells me that the "reader" is attempting to decipher my body language and is a con artist.

I once had a "reader" tell me that I was a recovering alcoholic, which was completely off the mark. She got rather nasty and I did not pay for her efforts.

A genuine psychic or medium will generally offer a refund if a client is not happy with a reading. However, a sitter may be unhappy due to a number of factors unrelated to the medium's reading. One possibility is that the medium correctly interpreted the message, and although the sitter validated this interpretation, he or she was not prepared to accept it. In these cases, the medium would be unlikely to offer a refund.

A medium working towards the greater good is acutely aware that the person might be vulnerable and will under no circumstances exploit that vulnerability.

I first asked myself the following two questions many years ago. Initially, I found the process extremely confrontational, since it meant being completely honest with myself. However, as time has passed and I have continued to pose these questions, I find my responses keep me grounded.

1. Before I die, will I need to apologise for an injustice I have done to someone? I hope not, so I endeavour to behave with integrity.

    When I need to apologise to a person, I will acknowledge I was in the wrong. I have taught myself not to allow pride to prevent me from saying sorry, and I then consciously observe my behaviour so that I do not repeat mistakes.

As for those from my childhood to whom I may have been unkind through lack of awareness, I have apologised to the universe, knowing that the vibration of my words would be sent through the ether to the intended person even when I am unable to recall a name.

2. What is the legacy that I will leave behind and that people will remember me by? For example, will they say that I was a kind person who helped and inspired others or that I was a greedy, manipulative bully? Whatever the question you ask, do it with honesty (which is harder than we realise!).

Interestingly, when I have put these questions to people in my private and working lives, the response is usually, "Does it really matter when I'm gone? I won't be able to say sorry by then, will I? And I won't know what people are saying about me anyway!"

My answer has always been the same. "Absolutely it does! Trust me when I tell you that you will definitely hear what people are saying about you. Why is this? Because you will seek out people like me to communicate your apologies to those you leave behind."

What then generally happens is that a spirit entity that a person can identify presents itself to prove what I have said. I always ask for permission to pass the message on, and often out of curiosity the person will say yes. When I do this, I am usually met with astonishment, or the individual will say, "You're freaking me out! There's no way you could have known that!"

What Fee Should I Charge?

What you charge for your services is entirely up to you. However, it is advisable to keep your fees affordable and within market rates so that you are accessible to everyone. You can have a sliding scale if you choose, allowing the less fortunate to have access to your services.

I once visited the MindBodySpirit Festival in Melbourne where I met and began chatting with a well-known medium who had become a media personality. I mentioned that I too was a practicing medium, and we began comparing our experiences. A prospective client approached the medium to enquire about fees for a reading, since she had seen the medium on TV and was a fan. The medium responded that her fee was $250 per hour. The woman said she was unable to afford that, but would love a reading with this medium. The medium immediately felt the need to justify the charge and declared, "I don't charge $250 an hour because I've been on TV and become well known."

I felt quite saddened and am convinced that my presence contributed to the medium's discomfort (even though I kept a poker face).

I was intrigued by her statement, since it indicated to me a deep sense of guilt over the cost. I read between the lines to learn what the medium was really saying, and although I could be wrong in my interpretation (I am neither a psychologist nor psychiatrist, though I am studying neuro linguistic programming and life coaching), I do not think I am mistaken. What I "heard" in her assertion was this.

> "OK, I've raised my prices since I became famous and I feel really bad about it! But I've been doing more readings than ever and it feels wonderful to have the money, and I don't want to do readings for people who say they can't afford it. But I can't help thinking that this is going to come back and bite me on the backside sooner or later."

Mediums have the right to re-evaluate the customers they wish to serve. That is not an issue. However, I find it interesting that a medium who prices herself far above market rates, and therefore beyond the reach of the general public, would then feel guilt over her decision. Why should the rich have to pay more than the poor? Why are the less fortunate unable to afford to have a reading with their chosen medium? I am not saying that mediums should not charge for their services. However, donating, say, three readings a year to those whose circumstances otherwise prevent them from accessing us might well relieve any shame over increasing our fees.

My philosophy as a practicing psychic medium is this: Remember where you came from. Appreciate what you have. Be accessible to those who need you. Maintain a level of humility.

This philosophy may not be for everyone, but it reminds me of my purpose in life.

I have always believed that psychics and mediums are doing what they do because they want to use their gifts to help people. I appreciate that they need to earn an income in an ever-fluctuating economy. (I am doing exactly that.) Nevertheless, if psychics and mediums are beyond the reach of those who cannot afford our fees and are not in a position to ask for help, we are no longer serving the greater good. Others may think differently.

The universe records when we are misusing our gifts, and karma will accumulate, whether we believe in it or not, and will eventually have to be settled. Our actions, good or bad, will often have consequences for us.

What goes around comes around. What goes around comes around, and comes around tenfold. Many people use these karmic sayings in everyday conversation. These adages have been proved true by global human experience, but even though we know the truth, we have an uncanny habit of ignoring it.

If we use adages such as these when speaking about others, we should be mindful of our own behaviour.

HOLISTIC HEALING

Holistic medicine has roots dating back approximately five thousand years to India and China. These ancient civilizations stressed healthy living and living in harmony with nature and believed that all parts of our being are connected and that no part can be treated in isolation.

Socrates taught that treating only one part of the body would produce poor results. Since all parts are interrelated, he said, healing should come as a whole. Hippocrates emphasised the body's ability to heal itself, and he was aware that there are many contributing factors to health, including the environment, the weather, the food we consume, and our emotional state.

What Is Holistic Medicine?

Holistic medicine, also known as holistic healing or holism, is not a method but an approach to wellness. The principle is treatment of the entire person, not just the pain or the disease. The aim is the improvement of a person's mental, physical, emotional, and spiritual well-being.

Holistic medicine is the art and science of healing that addresses the person's, mind, body, and spirit, and the practice integrates traditional and complementary therapies, promoting health and preventing and treating disease. This approach includes conventional medicine as well as alternative therapies. Holistic medicine covers all forms of diagnosis and treatment, including everything from prescription medicines to energy healing, acupuncture, chiropractic, and herbal remedies.

Although holistic practitioners prefer complementary and alternative methods whenever feasible, they are aware that at times traditional medicine is necessary. This may include surgery and prescription drugs if they are deemed the best approach to health issues.

Many holistic practitioners extend the definition of treatment to include education, personal responsibility, and love of self, which means caring about yourself enough to do what it takes to improve your health in all areas of your life.

Our physiology is continuously changing, which means our cells are altering too, and as we age, the cells we lose are not replaced. Sadly, we begin to show signs of age. Nevertheless, if we look after ourselves, the ageing process will slow. We can maintain our health, keeping the body resistant to disease, and with the use of holistic healing, regeneration of cells occurs not only externally but internally, making us feel healthier and stronger.

As with most natural remedies, occasionally a condition can worsen before it gets better. But this healing crisis is a temporary state, and the body's condition generally improves after adequate rest.

Complementary therapy should not be considered an alternative to professional medical advice. It can be used in conjunction with orthodox medicine. A person taking medication should consult with the prescribing professional prior to discontinuing use.

Some Healing Modalities

Aura Energy Healing

Aura energy healing clears and realigns the electromagnetic energy field (aura) surrounding the body and is aimed at ensuring our overall health and well-being.

This type of healing clears negative influences in each layer of the aura, allowing energy bodies to flow harmoniously. It is a gentle, nonintrusive (no touching is required), natural, and effective healing modality. Clients remain fully clothed, allowing them to feel secure and relaxed.

Aura energy healing is achieved by the movement of the healer's hands throughout the aura. Energy workers scan the body for imbalances, impurities, and/or blockages, identifying areas that need treatment and drawing healing energy from the universe without using their own vital energy. They realise that as instruments through which universal healing energies move, they must conduct the healing with unconditional love and light.

A healthy aura will feel smooth and free of blockages when healers run their hands through it. Blockages can be felt as cool or cold spots, warm or hot spots, and thick or sticky patches. By focussing and moving their hands over blocked areas, healers pick up unwanted energy and throw it away by vigorously shaking their hands. The process is repeated until the area feels clear of obstacles and healers sense they can move to the next site that needs clearing.

Here are the seven aura layers that surround the body. (See the section "Auras.")

- The first layer, the etheric body, is associated with the physical well-being of the human structure.
- The second layer, the emotional body, is related to our emotions.
- The third layer, the mental body, is connected to our psychological thought processes, ideas, and core values.
- The fourth layer, the astral body, is linked to our ability to love ourselves and others without condition.
- The fifth layer, the etheric template, is affiliated with all forms of communication. At this level, our higher selves can converse with the spiritual plane.
- The sixth layer, the celestial or intuitive body, is associated with our intuitive knowledge and spiritual awareness. This is the area where all our memories of our union with the universal one consciousness are stored.
- The seventh layer, the ketheric or causal template body, connects us to all knowledge held in the cosmos and is the association to our inner divine selves. It is the area where imprints of experiences throughout our many incarnations are preserved.

During a healing session, all aspects of our physical, emotional, mental, and spiritual health are being treated simultaneously. However, because everything in the body is connected, it is not uncommon for symptoms to be felt in areas that are not being treated at that moment. Consequently, during treatment the entire energy field rather than a specific area should receive care. When the aura is cleansed, the session is closed off, preventing the body from reverting to its previous state.

People who have received aura energy healing after surgery often find their recovery speeds up rapidly. A natural remedy, aura healing can be used in conjunction with traditional medical treatment.

Colour Therapy/Chromotherapy

Colour therapy/chromotherapy is an alternative therapy found in the ancient cultures of Egypt, China, and India and dates back thousands of years. Colour is light of varying wavelengths, which means that each colour has its own wavelength frequency and energy.

The energies relating to the seven bands of colours (red, orange, yellow, green, blue, indigo, and violet) resonate with the seven main energy centres (chakras) of the body. (See the section "Chakras.") Balancing the energy in our chakras is important for our overall health and well-being. Colour therapy can help to rebalance and/or stimulate these energies by applying the appropriate colour to the body, assisting in the realignment of our chakras. Red relates to the base chakra, orange to the sacral chakra, yellow to the solar plexus chakra, green to the heart chakra, blue to the throat chakra, indigo to the brow/third eye chakra, and violet to the crown chakra.

Visualise the chakras as spinning vortexes (like a tornado and its tail) that work like an engine. Each wheel must move smoothly for the engine to work properly. Similarly, good health and well-being are achieved by balancing all these energies to work in harmony with each other.

There are many ways of administering colour, including crystals, light boxes with colour filters, solarized water, and hands-on healing using colour.

In the section "Chakras," you will see our seven primary energy centres and their associated colours. Also included in that section are crystals and gemstones for use on each chakra along with descriptions of balanced and unbalanced chakras.

Colour affects us even as a foetus in the womb, where we are enveloped in nurturing pastels. When a woman is pregnant, it is quite normal for a psychic or medium to see pastel colours in the aura. The baby's gender may be determined by observing the most dominant pastel. Colour is associated with our earliest learning processes, and these associations contribute to our consciousness.

As we get older, we attach many feelings, memories, and meanings to colours, and this can become a feature of our subconscious. We can also build up prejudices to colours that have happy, sad, or frightening meanings for us.

All experiences make an impression upon us. Some will be positive and others negative, and the negative experiences can manifest themselves over time as disease or dis-ease.

Noting strong colour preferences or intolerances can be helpful in the discovery of possible issues, assist in the selection of appropriate colours to help dispel negative feelings, remove blockages, and rebalance the body emotionally, spiritually, physically, and mentally.

Colour therapy is safe to use alone or alongside any other therapy, be it conventional medicine or another complementary therapy.

Crystal and Gemstone Healing

Since the earliest times, crystals and gemstones have been used in ornaments and structures, creating what we call crystal therapy. Ancient records of crystal healing were discovered in Egyptian relics, among the most notable being the Ebers Papyrus,[10] which describes the therapeutic uses of many gems. Approximately five thousand years ago, this healing

---

[10] The Ebers Papyrus, a 110-page scroll about twenty meters long, is an Egyptian medical papyrus dated to circa 1550 BC. It is among the oldest preserved medical documents. New World Encyclopedia. 2011. Last modified April 2011. http://www.newworldencyclopedia.org/entry/Ebers_Papryus.

technique was also used in ancient Indian Ayurvedic[11] and traditional Chinese medicine. Native American tribes and Mayan and Aborigine people also used crystals for healing, meditation, and ceremonies.

Unfortunately, much valuable data explaining the development of crystal therapy has been lost through the years. However, more information on the origin of crystal therapy has been discovered, revealing the healing benefits.

Crystal therapy is the art of laying on stones. In crystal healing, stones are placed on the chakra points. A healer or therapist selects and arranges the gems, stones, and crystals to resonate the energy that will open the chakras. The energies delivered by the stones merge and correct imbalances in the chakras, encouraging the body to heal naturally.

Crystal healers believe that all living creatures have vibrational energy systems constructed by the chakras, the aura, and its subtle bodies and meridians. Ailments arise whenever there is an imbalance between these energies. Healers use various kinds of stones to tune the energy system and balance the body's inherent energies. The crystals used in healing are selected based on vibration, colour, chemical structure, and physical form, all of which influence the energy within and surrounding the body. A practitioner can move, focus, and direct imbalances of energy, using the structure of crystal for the body to imitate.

Crystal therapy works with an etheric grid lying beyond a human being's normal field of vision. When the body is surrounded with electromagnetic energies, placing crystals close to it can create a field of electricity capable of affecting the chakras. A crystal bearing the colour that resonates with a particular chakra can be used to accelerate the

---

[11]   Ayurveda is a medical science developed during the Vedic times, about five thousand years ago. Ayurveda means the "science of life" and is not only a medicinal system, but a way of life dealing with the physical and spiritual aspects of health. The medicinal form is governed by the laws of nature, which suggest that life is a combination of senses, mind, body, and soul. According to the science of life, every individual is composed of five elements: earth, water, fire, air, and space. iloveindia.com. 2012. "Ayurveda in India". Access date September 2012. http://www.ayurveda.iloveindia.com.

healing of its associated areas and organs by penetrating the subtle layers of the body's innate energies. This principle is known as "vibration and resonance." Since crystals create specific network patterns and various forms of sacred geometry, they can generate pillars of light that open chakras.

Crystal stones can prevent or remedy physical illnesses and symptoms. They are used to relieve severe and chronic conditions and anxiety and to facilitate preoperative care and postoperative healing. Crystals support recovery from ailments or symptoms by activating and encouraging the body's natural healing processes, and each stone has special and specific influences on the vibrational energies of the body.

Feather Healing

Feathers seem to be a natural conductor for energy, which means they contribute higher vibrations during healing, thus assisting in a speedier, more effective recovery.

Prior to deep feather healing, a person's aura must be scanned for blocked energy or hot or cold spots. Changes in the energy field are identified by running the hands three to seven inches away from the body.

Specific feathers are generally used for particular work. Brown turkey feathers, for instance, are used for work on the auric field. The rays in the brown colours of a turkey feather assist in grounding some people. A white feather, such as a turkey or a cockatoo feather, may be used when working on the individual chakras, providing a sense of connection with the one consciousness.

Two movements are required when working to enhance an energy field. Begin by using long sweeping and stroking movements to clear the main body of the aura. It is normal to feel strong initial resistance during a clearing. This is generally a result of the energy field being clogged by useless waste.

Sweeps with the feather should be slow when moving through the aura, and pressure should be constant yet gentle. Starting at the rear of the head, move the feather down the back, then down each leg. Then do the same for the sides and front of the body. Once the main body of the aura has been cleared, deep feather work can commence. This technique is used to treat specific problems, such as sore muscles. Use quick, choppy sweeps in a repeated format. The feather's energy draws the problem to the surface and helps disperse it. If the issue is close to the head, the method may have to be adapted depending on the person's sensitivity in this area. The shaft of the feather can be used to direct energy in a spiral motion to dislodge any blocks. This causes less stress while still dealing with the blocked energy.

The final step is opening the chakras. Holding a pendulum in your dominant hand (the hand you write with), dangle it over the chakra to assess its state. It should begin to spin in a circular motion, which may be perfectly round or oval, and the pendulum may swing too widely or too narrowly. Chakras should be roughly the size of a saucer. The pendulum can also be used to gauge the completion of the chakra alignment.

Using your nondominant hand (the hand you do not write with), place the shaft of the feather on each chakra, channelling the energy into the opening. Dangle the pendulum above the top of the feather, and the pendulum should gain momentum as the feather revitalises, revealing when the chakra is completely open. This process can take various lengths of time, but generally, it should not last any more than a few minutes per chakra. Feather healers can tell when the chakras are open through a variety of signals. For me, that signal comes when the pendulum spins consistently for a few minutes over a specific circumference and then stops or slows significantly.

Music Healing Therapy

Music therapy has gone through some exciting shifts in the last couple of decades. These changes have been driven by insights from research into music and brain function.

Biomedical researchers have found that music is a structured auditory language involving complex perception, cognition, and motor control in the brain. Therefore it can be used to re-educate the brain.[12]

---

[12] The Dana Foundation: 2010. "How Music Helps to Heal the Injured Brain:

Therapists and physicians now use music in rehabilitation, employing methods that are not only supported by clinical research but are endorsed by knowledge of the mechanisms of music and brain function.

Developments in music research have been applied to neurologic therapy over the past decade. Music therapy has progressed from soft science or no science to hard science, and neurologic music therapy meets the standards of evidence-based medicine.

Research has demonstrated that music has a profound effect on the body and the psyche, and those who practice music therapy are discovering that music is advantageous when used with cancer patients and children with attention deficit disorder. Hospitals are using music therapy to aid in pain management, deflecting depression, encouraging movement, relaxing patients, and easing muscle tension.[13]

Here are some of the effects of music, which help explain the success of music therapy.

1. Brainwaves

Research shows that music with a strong beat can excite brainwaves to resonate in harmony with the rhythm. Faster beats bring sharper concentration, and a slower tempo encourages a calm, meditative state. It has also been established that the change in brainwave activity levels that music can cause allows the brain to change its rate of motion more easily. This means that even after an individual has stopped listening, music can benefit his state of mind.

2. Heart Rate and Breathing

Changes in brainwaves help modify other bodily functions. Those directed by the nervous system, such as breathing and heart rate, can be altered by the changes music produces. This can mean a

---

Therapeutic Use Crescendos Thanks to Advances in Brain Science" by Michael Thaut, Ph.D. and Gerald McIntosh, M.D. March 2010. http://www. dana.org/news/cerebrum/detail.aspx?id=26122

[13] About.com. 2011. "Stress Management: How and Why Music is A Good Tool for Health" by Elizabeth Scott, M.S. October 2011. http://stress.about. com/od/tensiontamers/a/music_therapy.htm

slower heart rate, slower breathing, and activation of the relaxation response, resulting in counteraction or prevention of the damaging effects of chronic stress, which in turn promotes health and well-being.

3. State of Mind

Music can be used to encourage a positive state of mind and to help ward off depression and anxiety, preventing the stress response from causing pandemonium in the body.

4. Other Benefits

Music has been found to bring many other benefits, such as lowering blood pressure (reducing the risk of stroke and other health problems), improving immunity, and easing muscle tension. With the many advantages and profound physical effects that it brings, music is an important instrument in helping the body to stay or become healthy.

Reiki

Reiki was accepted in its current form at the end of the nineteenth century by Doctor Mikao Usui, a Japanese Buddhist monk, who, after extensive research into ancient scriptures, spent twenty-one days fasting and meditating on a holy mountain, focussing on sacred symbols and mantras that he found in Buddhist texts. It is said that on the twenty-first day, after seeing these symbols in his mind, each enclosed by a brilliant golden light, Usui realised that he had changed forever.

Following this experience, Usui discovered that if he laid his hands on an individual suffering discomfort, the person would rapidly feel better. He decided that he should pass these skills on. Thus he created the accepted model of teaching and practice used today.

Usui found that by using the symbols in a specific way, he could transmit the energy to others so that they too could begin healing. However, after some years spent serving the poor in Kyoto, Usui observed that they frequently did not take advantage of their newly gifted well-being, so he decided that to be effectively healed, those who received reiki had to have a genuine wish to be helped. Usui moved to a clinic in Tokyo, and in partnership with Chijuro Hayashi, a medical doctor, established the foundation for all reiki forms that have followed.

What is Reiki?

Reiki is a Japanese word made up of two words: *rei,* meaning "universal," and *ki,* meaning "life force." Reiki is the energy that creates everything around and within us, and is a simple and practical method for deep relaxation and hands-on healing. Through reiki training, a direct connection can be made with the limitless supply of universal energy that surrounds us. We can draw it in when applying our hands to ourselves or another person. This mode of healing rebalances us on all levels of the mind, body, spirit, and emotions.

When we administer reiki to another person, the energy flows unencumbered through us and not from us. It then enters the receiver, and we do not give away any of our own vital energy in the process.

The Four Degrees/Stages of Reiki

Reiki is taught by a master level-two teacher and is divided into four degrees or stages. There are intervals between each course, allowing students to attain a greater understanding of what they have learned before advancing to the next level.

Reiki First Degree

This level is for those who want to understand reiki and activate their ability to heal themselves, family members, friends, babies, children, and animals.

Reiki Second Degree

This level is for those who have completed their reiki first degree and wish to extend their reiki practice and understanding, and includes learning how to perform distance healing.

Reiki Master Level One

This course is for the person who wishes to find spiritual enlightenment and achieve personal awareness. Progression to this level requires a strong commitment to regular self-healing, which will lead to a more profound understanding of universal energy and the meaning of knowledge.

Reiki Master Level Two—Teacher

This level is for experienced practitioners who have completed all the other levels and wish to pass on their reiki learning to others. Training requires immense dedication, since it can take several years to complete.

EARTH WORK

What is Earth Work?

T his is an interesting topic, since we all have our own views about what constitutes spiritual earth work. Discovering what it means to you is 90 percent of the challenge. For me, it meant finding some form of balance between my human self and my spirit self. When I achieved that goal, I ceased pouring into Mother Earth and her atmosphere the negativity I felt. That cascading waterfall of toxic waste that I passed on to the world was no more. As I made giant changes in my life, I found my hand chakras activated, and I needed to expend the enormous build-up of energy in them. It seemed logical to me that if no one was willing to accept this energy (my husband kept telling me to stop touching him!), then Mother Earth would be happy to receive it.

I placed my hands on the ground and could feel the energy pulsating through them to this great planet that provides for us. I felt relieved, and interestingly enough, I sensed little rumblings coming from under my feet. I became more in tune with Mother Nature, and simply by changing my attitude and sending my excess energy into her (even on a small scale), I felt like I was contributing to this tragically ravaged planet in a positive way.

I began to see portals (I believe these are gateways to other dimensions, though I am not sure) opening in our local park. They presented themselves as great flashes of white light that swirled as they formed in front of me. They had an iridescence about them, but appeared to be translucent white. As I walked through them, I would instantly be transported out of my body for a few seconds and would immediately feel at peace and cleansed before returning.

I haven't been able to fully identify why these portals form. However, I simply accept that they are there. I knew this was not an offer to return to spirit. I simply became more in tune with the earth's electromagnetic energies and realised that to connect with the divine, I needed to first connect with the earth. When I did that, the pathway of communication with my higher self, the spirit, and our creator became so much easier.

So earth work, as my truth speaks, is about finding equilibrium between our material world and our spiritual world by first reconnecting to the planet that so generously shares her life force with us.

By sending our healing energy into the earth, we allow ourselves to recognise and be grateful for what we are being given by a very kind benefactor, Mother Earth.

CRYSTALS

Having always been attracted to the beautiful colours emitted by crystals, I did not realise their real uses until my hand chakras activated. As I started becoming self-aware and noticed their fine vibrations in my hands, I found particular crystals seemed to calm me when I was stressed or anxious. This led me to use them when healing myself, and I would instinctively place them on certain points of my body when lying down. My body would then rapidly settle into a state of balance, encouraging my mind to slow down. When I reached this state, my mind, body, and spirit began healing, and over time, these aspects of self merged, offering a greater understanding of who I really am.

What Are Crystals?

Crystals are solid matter in which atoms are arranged in regular geometrical shapes that were created as our planet formed. They change as the earth evolves, recording all the alterations of each phase of evolution, and they hold enormous amounts of information on the earth's structure.

The shape of a crystal is determined by the mineral's atomic arrangement. Crystals have recognisable structures that have been affected by temperature, pressure, chemical conditions, and the amount of space in which they form.

Many develop in moist environments that may be underground or on the surface of the planet; some might form during volcanic eruptions when lava quickly cools. Table salt and sugar are everyday materials you encounter as crystals. Many gemstones, including quartz and diamond, are crystals.

Some Commonly Used Crystals

Amethyst

The amethyst is transparent and purple to lavender in colour and is an excellent crystal for absorbing negativity in hostile environments. It must be placed outside during a full moon so that the negativity absorbed can be cleared. It is associated with the brow/third eye and crown chakras, although most commonly with the crown chakra.

Healing Properties

The amethyst is said to lessen pain, bruising, and inflammation. It can strengthen the immune system and can be used to treat hearing disorders and to boost the nervous system. It is also beneficial in stimulating the healing of the heart, stomach, and digestive tract.

The stone is both calming and stimulating to the mind, depending on what is needed. It allows greater focus and control of the faculties, enabling a person to feel less scattered, thereby promoting integration of new ideas.

The amethyst assists in curing fears produced by nightmares, which can often lead to insomnia. The crystal has reportedly been used for protection against overindulgence in alcohol and to fight addictions. The amethyst is known to calm the mind and to promote emotional centering by dispelling anger, fear, and anxiety.

A stone of spiritual protection and purification, the amethyst teaches and encourages humility. It promotes love of the divine and encourages altruism and wisdom, allowing a person to connect with his intuition and to discover his true self. The amethyst helps convert low vibrations to higher energies.

Black Tourmaline

The black tourmaline is a shiny, opaque or transparent, long-striated,[14] hexagonally structured crystal. This stone offers extremely good protection against electromagnetic smog,[15] mobile phones, computers, radiation, psychic attack, and hexes. Placed point out from the body, the black tourmaline will draw off negative energy. It is associated with the first chakra, known as the base/root chakra.

Healing Properties

The black tourmaline protects against incapacitating ailments, strengthens the immune system, treats arthritis, provides pain relief, and helps readjustment of the spine.

The stone clears destructive thoughts, encourages an easy-going outlook on life, and objectivity with clear, balanced thought. It arouses humanitarianism and creativity. It encourages balance between the left and right sides of the brain, which helps in understanding yourself and those around you, and improves hand-eye coordination. By balancing the energy in the body and aiding in elimination of toxins, the black tourmaline can banish stress, calm anxiety, and promote emotional stability.

The black tourmaline is a shamanic stone that brings protection during rituals. It keeps a person grounded and protects astral travellers during meditation. It is one the best stones to wear for protection.

Bloodstone

The bloodstone is a variety of deep green chalcedony that in the past was called heliotrop. The word *heliotrop* is derived from two Greek words: *helios*, meaning "the sun," and *tropos*, meaning "to turn." This

---

[14] A striated rock is one with a number of parallel lines or scratches on the surface.

[15] Electromagnetic smog is a subtle yet measurable electromagnetic field produced by televisions, mobile phones, computers, and electrical power lines.

green quartz has spots or patches of red or yellow jasper within it. The red spots are iron oxide that resemble the colour of blood, giving the stone its name. The bloodstone is associated with the blood of Christ, since it was believed to have formed when some of Jesus's blood fell during his crucifixion, staining jasper that lay at the foot of the cross. The bloodstone links the base/root chakra with the heart chakra.

Healing Properties

The bloodstone helps cleanse the blood, enhancing blood flow and circulation. It is used to treat anaemia and ease menstrual and menopausal symptoms. The bloodstone benefits the immune system, heart, liver, kidneys, intestines, and bladder and neutralises toxins in the body. It invigorates the lymphatic system and minimises pus formation, helping to heal infection and inflammation.

The stone calms and revitalises the mind when a person is mentally exhausted. It enhances decision making and eliminates confusion. Bloodstones are also known as stones of courage and help people avoid dangerous situations. The stone enhances creativity and promotes idealism and selflessness.

The bloodstone alleviates grief, lifts the spirit, increases confidence and self-love, calms anxiety, prevents jealousy, and reduces hostility and irritability.

Dubbed an "audible oracle," the bloodstone was said to deliver its predictions through sounds, such as cracking. It heightens intuition, stimulates dreaming, and encourages the wearer to act in the present moment. It has been said that bloodstones carry properties that enable a person to control the weather[16] and that they have the ability to banish evil and negativity. Connection with past lives can be facilitated by holding a bloodstone during meditation.

---

[16] I have seen no evidence of this, but that does not mean it has not happened when someone else has used the stone for that purpose.

Blue Lace Agate

The blue lace agate is generally a tumbled stone with banded (striped) layers, usually in the lighter blue shades. However, the stone can come with whites, brighter blues, and brown threads of colour seen within the layers. It is associated with the throat chakra.

Healing Properties

This crystal is used to treat infections and sore throats. It also lowers fevers and eliminates obstructions in the nervous system. The blue lace agate is said to decrease bone inflammation, which reinforces the skeleton, aiding the healing of fractures.

The blue lace agate encourages authenticity and practical thinking and has a calming and cooling energy that brings peace of mind, which assists in counteracting anger. It aids the expression of thoughts and feelings through verbal communication. This stone is excellent for those who communicate for a living, such as teachers and lecturers, and helps to calm the nerves when a person is called upon to speak in public.

This crystal helps counteract fear-based emotions produced when we feel we are being rejected or judged. It is beneficial in self-reflection, revealing concealed situations that may hinder our emotional well-being. It encourages self-acceptance and confidence, inspiring us to speak our own truth. The blue lace agate overcomes negativity and resentment by healing anger and frustration, thereby promoting love.

When used for inner attunement, the blue lace agate helps us to reach a high level of spiritual awareness by connecting us to the collective conscious. It links our thoughts to the higher vibrations of our spiritual energy, allowing us to feel peace. Because this stone is associated with the throat chakra, it helps clear blockages within this energy body, permitting our highest spiritual truths to be expressed.

Calcite

Calcite is a waxy crystal that comes in blue, brown, grey, green, orange, pink, red, and yellow. It is a protecting, grounding, and centering stone that assists in finding inner peace. As a powerful amplifier and cleanser of energy, calcite will clear negative energies from a room.

This stone can be used to open and balance all the chakras.

Healing Properties

Calcite is good for back pain, teeth, and eyes. It can be used to increase strength and to detoxify the body, and it is also an antiseptic agent. Calcite has been associated with the bones and the joints and can help balance the amount of calcium retained by the body and dissolve calcifications, strengthening the skeleton. It fortifies the immune system, alleviating intestinal and skin problems. Calcite can also help improve the absorption of vitamins and minerals. Orange calcite can assist in treatment of the reproductive system, the gallbladder, and intestinal ailments.

The stone encourages positivity and personal motivation by connecting the emotions with the intellect, promoting emotional intelligence. Calcite calms the mind and is known as the "stone of the mind" because it heightens good mental judgement and increases memory capacity. Students can benefit from having calcite near them, since the stone increases learning abilities and drive.

Calcite is particularly useful in alleviating stress and is generally considered good for balancing male/female energies and emotions, allowing us to freely express our feelings.

This is a stone of spirituality, wisdom, and reconciliation. Calcite increases intuition and is helpful in astral travel and channelling. It is also a good choice for conducting distance healing work, since it amplifies the energy being sent.

Carnelian

The carnelian is a translucent, often water-worn stone that comes in brown, orange, red, and pink. It is a stone of ambition and drive, which makes it useful for career choices, since it promotes concrete decisions. This stone provides additional energy when a person feels tired or run— down. It is connected to the base/root, sacral, and heart chakras.

Healing Properties

The carnelian aids in the absorption of vitamins, minerals, and nutrients. It influences the female reproductive organs, increasing fertility and easing menstrual cramps. It cleanses the blood, regulates the kidneys, relieves lower back pain, and when applied to the body, promotes balanced digestion and is said to aid in detoxification.

This stone promotes courage and dispels lethargy, motivating us to be successful in our endeavours. It stimulates analytical abilities and attention to detail, promoting the rediscovery or discovery of talents by inspiring curiosity. It balances our creativity with our psychological processes.

The carnelian calms our fears about death, bringing peace and acceptance of the cycle of life, which includes death and rebirth. It helps overcome grief and depression, promoting optimism by encouraging us to enjoy life. The carnelian protects from all negative emotions, particularly rage, envy, fear, lethargy, and inaction. It helps overcome the fear of public speaking, making the speaker feel relaxed and self-assured and so encouraging eloquence.

As a grounding crystal, the carnelian is excellent for those who feel like space cadets because they have spent too much time in the higher chakras (crown, brow/third eye, and throat chakras). By creating a balance between the worlds of spirit and earth, the carnelian helps the individual enjoy and appreciate both aspects of living.

Celestite

Celestite is a transparent, pyramidal cluster of crystals, or geodes,[17] that ranges in size, coming in blue, red, yellow, and white. This stone is infused with celestial energies, and its high vibration brings stability and alignment. Celestite is generally associated with the brow/third

---

[17]   A geode is a small, hollow, usually rounded rock lined on the inside with inward-pointing crystals. Geodes form when mineral-rich water entering a cavity in a rock undergoes a sudden change in pressure or temperature, causing crystals to form from the solution and line the cavity's walls.

eye chakra, but I have used it on the throat chakra, finding it beneficial when the need to communicate clearly has arisen.

Healing Properties

Celestite is known to ease tension in the body by eliminating toxins. It relieves headaches, treats eye and ear ailments and digestive problems, helps alleviate sore throats, and assists in regulating the thyroid gland.

The stone calms and sharpens the mind, promoting mental balance, and encourages harmonious coexistence with others.

As a calming stone, it soothes a quick temper, supporting compassion and healing. This crystal promotes purity of heart and attracts good fortune. Celestite teaches us to recognise our quiet strength by inspiring inner peace.

Celestite encourages enlightenment, revealing personal truths. It helps cleanse the aura and aids clairvoyance, out-of-body experiences, and dream recall. Meditation with this crystal assists in angelic communication when channelling. Celestite inspires trust in recognising and accepting that we are part of the divine plan. It is said that astral travellers can use celestite to improve their precision in reaching their chosen destinations.

Citrine

The citrine is a transparent quartz that comes in all sizes and is yellow to yellowish-brown or a smoky grey-brown. It does not absorb negative energy from its surroundings, so it does not need to be cleansed or recharged. Known as the lucky "merchant's stone," a citrine is ideal to carry if you are in any type of sales. As a stone of abundance, it teaches us how to manifest wealth and prosperity. Place it in the wealth corner of your home or business, which is the point farthest back to the left from the front door or the door into a room.

This beautiful crystal carries the power of the sun, which makes it exceptionally beneficial as a purifier and regenerator of energy. The citrine transmutes, disperses, and grounds negative energy. It is associated with the sacral, solar plexus, and crown chakras.

Healing Properties

The citrine can increase visual abilities and help relieve insomnia and nightmares. It is beneficial to the endocrine, digestive, and circulatory systems. This crystal is useful for treatment of the thyroid, heart, kidney, liver, and urinary tract, and strengthens the immune system by cleansing, purifying, and eliminating built-up toxins.

The stone encourages creativity, enhances individuality, promotes motivation and honesty, and raises self-confidence by removing self-limiting tendencies. It invigorates the mind and improves the ability to focus, boosting the capacity to absorb information.

The citrine relieves depression, insecurity, anger, and mood swings. The stone encourages happiness in those who carry it and reduces self-destructive tendencies. The citrine assists in eliminating fears by helping the individual overcome grief, depression, phobias, and emotional trauma. It is said that sensuality and sexuality can also be intensified by citrine.

The citrine brings the virtues of self-healing, inspiration, and self-improvement, making it useful in promoting personal and spiritual awareness. This stone also activates and opens the crown chakra, allowing for easier communication with the higher self. The citrine protects and clears the aura of negative energies and influences and is particularly good in cleansing the sacral and solar plexus chakras. It is an excellent stone for dream recall and dream work.

Diamond

The diamond is a clear, transparent gemstone when cut and polished. It comes in a variety of colours, including blue, brown, clear white, yellow, and pink. It is the symbol of purity and is seen as a mark of commitment and loyalty. For aeons, the diamond has been deemed a stone of manifestation, attracting abundance. This comes from mankind's view that it is the stone of wealth. The diamond is considered to be a master healing stone and as an amplifier of energy is excellent at enhancing the power of other crystals around it during healing. Although the diamond is associated with the crown chakra, it has a harmonising influence on all the chakras.

Healing Properties

The diamond is said to treat glaucoma and aid in clearing sight. It rebalances the metabolism and treats allergies.

This stone will help combat mental illness when placed on the brow chakra. It benefits the brain, bringing clarity of mind, and aids enlightenment by clearing psychological and emotional pain, which diminishes anxiety. The diamond is a stone of creativity that inspires the imagination and encourages originality. The qualities that the diamond teaches include courage, strength, and resilience. This gemstone supports self-confidence and the desire for independence whilst diminishing jealousy.

The diamond is said to increase all energies within the mind, body, and spirit, assisting the alignment of these bodies by activating the crown chakra, linking it with the higher self.

Emerald

Emeralds are a form of beryl, originating from chromium impurities within the crystal structure. They are generally vibrant green and come tumbled, cut, or as cloudy crystals. When cut and polished, the emerald is seen as a valuable gemstone. It is considered to be a stone of love and romance, bringing and enhancing joy, unity, and unconditional love, and promoting friendship. The emerald has long been the symbol of faith and hope and is considered by many to be the stone of prophecy. It is associated with the heart chakra.

Healing Properties

The emerald treats the sinuses, lungs, heart, spine, and muscles. It soothes and strengthens the eyes, improves the immune and nervous systems, alleviates rheumatism and diabetes, and aids recovery after infectious illness.

This stone provides strength to overcome misfortunes. The emerald calms a troubled mind and is said to bring the wearer reason and wisdom.

The emerald benefits intuition and communication, promotes honesty, and inspires profound inner knowing. It draws to the surface of the psyche what we know on an unconscious level but have yet to discover. The emerald is a stone of patience and inspiration and encourages these attributes in the wearer.

Fluorite

Pure fluorite is clear, yet other minerals frequently combine with it, so fluorite is found in a wide range of colours, including blue, green, purple, yellow, and brown. It can be transparent, giving it a glassy look, and comes in cubic or octahedral[18] crystals of all sizes. Interestingly, this stone is often fluorescent under UV lighting, producing a mixture of colours. Fluorite cleanses and stabilises the aura and is extremely effective in combating electromagnetic stress from the environment, particularly computers and mobile phones. It is associated with the heart, throat, and brow/third eye chakras.

Healing Properties

Positioned on an affected area, fluorite eliminates discomfort. Direct application of the stone is also exceptionally helpful for disorders such as energy blockages, breathing issues, weeping wounds, skin complaints, and arthritis. It is said to benefit bones and teeth and to repair DNA damage at a cellular level.

Fluorite increases self-confidence and disperses self-limiting behavioural patterns by gently bringing suppressed emotions to the surface for clearing. It increases mental and physical harmony, neutralises psychological ailments, and helps a person to move past

---

[18] An octahedron is any polyhedron having eight plane faces. A polyhedron is a solid figure with many plane faces, typically more than six.

blinkered viewpoints by dissolving misconceptions and revealing the truth. Fluorite has a calming effect that supports an understanding of the effects of the emotions and the mind on the body. Since this crystal affects the intellectual mind, it assists in overcoming strong emotions and soothes feelings of desperation or depression.

Fluorite expands the mind to greater ideas, opening the wearer to new perceptions when old ones are of no more service. It is the crystal of the expanding mind.

Garnet

Garnets can appear transparent or be larger opaque stones. They come in a wide variety of colours including purple, red, orange, yellow, green, brown, or black, although they're generally thought of as red.

Garnets are excellent stones for manifestation, assisting with building positive self-image and with professional success. The garnet is commonly known as the stone for a successful business. Placing three or more garnets on your desk will encourage a fruitful business enterprise. The stone is also beneficial during a crisis, since it is especially supportive when life has become disjointed or particularly distressing. It is associated with the base chakra.

Healing Properties

The garnet is associated with the thyroid and spleen, and both organs may benefit from cleansing when the gemstone is held over them. It stimulates the metabolism and regenerates the body, renews DNA, assists the absorption of minerals and vitamins into the body, and cleanses and revitalises the blood, heart, and lungs. The garnet treats spinal and cellular disorders.

This stone is connected with the pituitary gland and can help improve insights into the self and others by encouraging greater self-awareness. It dissolves deep-rooted self-defeating behaviour patterns, or unconscious self-sabotage, and helps alleviate depression. It is said that the garnet will bring positive thoughts and boost energy.

The garnet is used to enhance sensuality, sexuality, and intimacy by removing inhibitions and restrictions. The stone opens the heart to romantic love and passion and provides confidence.

Holding a garnet whilst meditating on past lives can spur personal revelations, which may include past life recall. This crystal is believed to protect the wearer from negative energies and to send those energies back to the originator, which makes it an excellent stone for protection against psychic attack and malicious gossip.

Jade

Jade is the name of two gems with similar characteristics. The first is jadeite, and the second is nephrite. The two stones were recognised separately in 1863, and although nephrite is more common, both are hard, small-grained rocks suitable for carving.

Jadeite is made up of intertwining, coarse pyroxene[19] crystals, which come in a wide range of colours, including green, lilac, white, pink, brown, red, blue, black, orange, and yellow. The most valued variety, imperial jade, is a deep, rich emerald green due to chromium content. Jadeite commonly has a dimpled surface when polished.

Nephrite is found as collections of fibrous amphibole[20] crystals. This compound forms an interlocking structure that makes it tougher than steel. Colours can vary from a dark green (rich in iron content) to a cream colour (high in magnesium content). Nephrite jade may be banded, blotchy, or consistent in colour.

---

[19] Pyroxene refers to any of a group of silicate minerals having the general formula $ABSi_2O_6$. A is usually calcium, sodium, magnesium, or iron, and B is usually magnesium, iron, chromium, manganese, or aluminum. Pyroxenes occur in basic igneous rocks and some metamorphic rocks and have colours ranging from white to dark green or black. They may be monoclinic (clinopyroxenes) or orthorhombic (orthopyroxenes) in crystal structure. Examples are augite (the most important pyroxene), diopside, enstatite, hypersthene, and jadeite.

[20] Amphibole refers to any of a class of rock-forming silicate or aluminosilicate minerals typically occurring as fibrous or columnar crystals.

In Chinese tradition, jade represented the five virtues of humanity: wisdom, compassion, justice, modesty, and courage, which were often carved into the stone.

Jade is the sign of virtue and peacefulness, indicating wisdom gained in tranquillity. It is a protective crystal that keeps the wearer from harm, warding off negative energies, and creates harmony. It is said to promote courage, compassion, justice, generosity, humility, wealth, and longevity, leading to a richer, more rewarding life. It is associated with the heart chakra.

Healing Properties

Jade strengthens the heart, kidneys, adrenal glands, and nervous and immune systems, balances fluids within the body, encourages health in the organs that cleanse the blood, assists with fertility and childbirth, and works on the hips and spleen.

The stone merges the mind with the body by helping the personality to stabilise so that integration can be achieved.

Jade is called the "dream stone" for its capacity to produce insightful dreams. The stone supports emotional release, targeting impatience in particular.

It encourages wearers to recognise themselves as spiritual beings by drawing to the surface hidden knowledge.

Lapis Lazuli

Lapis lazuli is a veined stone that is deep blue and flecked with gold. It is protective and aids in contacting spirit guides and guardians. It teaches the power of the spoken word and is said to have the ability to reverse curses. Lapis lazuli recognises psychic attack, intercepts it, and sends the negative energy back to the originator.

Physicians in ancient Egypt, Sumer, and Babylon used lapis lazuli for medicinal purposes, which included healing eye cataracts. The connection with the eye might have come from the use of lapis lazuli in designs on carvings called *The Eye of Isis* or *The All-Seeing Eye of the Goddess Maat*. Since Isis was said to watch over the dead on their final journey, the lapis lazuli eye was placed in the sarcophagus with the mummy. The chief justice of Egypt wore the "eye of Maat" when he rendered judgements. The stone is associated with the brow/third eye chakra.

Healing Properties

Lapis lazuli relieves sore throats and inflammations of the neck and the head, particularly migraines. It is beneficial to the respiratory, nervous and immune systems, the throat, larynx, thyroid, and thymus. This stone aids in treatment of the ears, particularly hearing loss, cleanses the blood, relieves insomnia and vertigo, and lowers blood pressure.

The stone brings freedom from emotional slavery by stimulating emotional and mental clarity, offering profound insight into life. Lapis lazuli is associated with truth, balance, and justice and promotes determination and courage. It encourages serenity and self-acceptance, drawing anxieties to the surface for resolution. Lapis lazuli is a powerful thought amplifier and encourages the advanced abilities of the mind, creating open-mindedness and clarity. It aids in the expression of emotions, and bonds relationships in love and friendship. It is extremely useful for diffusing distress and malice.

Lapis lazuli encourages enlightenment and heightens dream work and psychic abilities. It facilitates spiritual exploration, increases personal and spiritual power, and stimulates and promotes total self-awareness. The energy of this stone is extremely high. Lapis lazuli does not lower its power to meet ours; rather, we must raise our mental, emotional, and spiritual energies to connect with lapis lazuli.

Obsidian

Obsidian is a shiny, opaque, naturally created glass formed from volcanic lava that cooled rapidly when it came in contact with water, preventing significant crystallisation. It is most often black, but obsidian also comes in brown, blue, grey-green, rainbow, red-black, silver, and gold-sheen and may be uniform, mottled, or banded in colour.

It is a very powerful stone and reminds us that birth and death coexist. It is a stone with no restrictions and works extremely quickly, with enormous power. Its insightful, truth-enhancing qualities are ruthless in revealing shortcomings, weaknesses, and blockages. Obsidian is associated with guardian spirits and is connected to protection on all levels. It is an exceptionally powerful stone and should be used with care, particularly if a person is extremely vulnerable. It is associated with the first chakra, known as the base chakra.

Healing Properties

Obsidian is said to alleviate pain, stop bleeding, benefit circulation, reduce tension, and release blocked energy. It helps disorders of the stomach and intestines, aiding digestion. The stone accelerates the healing of wounds and reduces the pain of arthritis and cramps. It is believed that obsidian can be used to shrink an inflamed prostate.

The stone encourages identification of behaviour patterns that no longer serve us, promoting recognition of who we truly are. It clears confusion, bringing clarity of thought.

Obsidian disperses blockages and old traumas, adding depth and clarity to feelings and encouraging empathy and strength. This stone brings repressed feelings to the surface for resolution.

The stone grounds spiritual energy in the physical plane and connects the mind and emotions. It absorbs and destroys negative energies and cleanses the unconscious and subconscious of blockages, releasing stress. Because obsidian energises spiritual forces and connects with the first chakra, it can assist in facing present challenges as well as past life lessons still to be learned. The third eye is frequently activated when processing past life karma, so obsidian should be used with caution.

Rhodochrosite

Rhodochrosite is an elegant pink—and white-banded stone called the "stone of love and balance" because it balances and enhances love on all levels. It also comes in orange and is associated with the heart chakra.

Healing Properties

Rhodochrosite regulates and stabilises the heart rate, balances blood pressure, stimulates circulation, kidneys, and reproductive organs. It alleviates migraines, skin disorders, thyroid imbalances, and intestinal problems. Rhodochrosite purifies the circulatory system and restores poor eyesight.

The stone encourages a positive attitude, creativity, and innovation and enhances dream states that give clarity to our questions.

Rhodochrosite stimulates love and passion, while energising the soul. It opens the heart, lifts depression, and encourages a positive outlook on life, improving self-worth by soothing emotional stress.

The stone expands consciousness and integrates spiritual and material energies. It attracts a soulmate to the wearer, but the relationship may not be what the wearer imagined, since the soulmate often arrives to teach this person lessons.

Rose Quartz

Rose quartz is a translucent crystal that derives its name from its lovely rose pink colour. Often called the "love stone," it teaches the meaning of unconditional love and opens the heart chakra to all forms of love: self-love, romantic love, family love, and platonic love. The high energy of this crystal gives it the ability to enhance love in virtually any situation. It is said that this stone can remind us of our purpose, promoting receptiveness to all kinds of beauty within and around us. Rose quartz gently draws off destructive energy in relationships, replacing it with loving feelings. It is associated with the heart chakra.

Healing Properties

Rose quartz can help heal the heart, the circulatory system, headaches and migraines, kidneys, adrenals, sinus and throat problems, depression, addictions, and earaches. It can slow the signs of ageing, reducing wrinkles, spleen problems, fibromyalgia, and thymus, fertility, and sexual dysfunction. It is helpful to those who suffer senile dementia and Alzheimer's and Parkinson's disease. Rose quartz also provides protection during pregnancy and childbirth.

The stone supports brain functions and increases intellect. It encourages positive affirmations, but it is a feeling stone and works best when used to heal our emotions.

Rose quartz brings gentleness, forgiveness, compassion, kindness, and tolerance. It raises self-esteem and self-respect and aids in balancing the emotions, healing emotional traumas, and bringing peace and calm. Rose quartz removes fears, resentments, and anger. It can also heal and release childhood sufferings, abandonment, and lack of love by enhancing inner awareness. It can promote reconciliation with family and with others. Overwhelming or unreasonable guilt is eased by rose quartz.

Rose quartz is often used to attract love. It is also used to ease the transition when dying. The stone can aid dream recall and dream work.

Turquoise

Turquoise is an opaque, often veined stone that comes in turquoise, blue, or green. Egyptians prized turquoise as a "life stone," and the oldest pieces of jewellery set with this gem are four bracelets found on the mummified arm of Queen Zar, who ruled Egypt around 5500 BC.

Turquoise is considered to be a symbol of generosity, sincerity, and affection, dispelling negative energy, and can be worn to protect against outside influences or pollutants in the atmosphere. It is a symbol of friendship and stimulates romantic love. It preserves friendships and can make friends out of enemies in time. Traditionally it is said to bring good luck only if given, not purchased. It is associated with the throat chakra.

Healing Properties

Turquoise assists in the absorption of nutrients, enhances the immune system, and stimulates the renewal of tissue, healing the entire body. It contains anti-inflammatory and purifying properties and eases cramps and pain. Turquoise cleanses the lungs, soothes and clears sore throats, and heals the eyes. It neutralises unhealthy levels of acidity, benefits rheumatism, gout, abdominal problems, and viral illnesses.

The stone balances and aligns all the chakras, stabilising mood swings and inspiring peace. It is excellent for fighting despair and fatigue and averting panic attacks. Turquoise promotes self-fulfilment, assists creative problem solving, and calms the nerves of those speaking in public.

As a meditation tool, turquoise can assist in clearing the mind, allowing a person insights into the universe. The stone adjusts the wearer's vibration to the spiritual plane and provides protection during vision quests or astral travel. Some Native American Indians call turquoise the "sky stone" or the "stone of heaven" and believe that vibrations from this crystal can bridge the gap between the material world and the spirit realm, giving strong psychic powers to the carrier. Turquoise is considered to be a power stone that strengthens and aligns all the chakras.

Reincarnation and Past Lives

During a meditation in 2011, I had a vision, including physical sensations, of an orphaned eight-year-old boy being burnt at the stake for cursing his village by bringing plague and death. I was not given a place or a time frame, but the boy appeared to be filthy and the words "street urchin" came to me. I felt enormous fear and distress, and the violence I saw and felt was sickening. I quickly brought my awareness back to the room where I was sitting and found my face drenched in tears.

I decided to investigate what I saw. For the next few days I focussed only on that event during meditation. The same scene kept presenting itself. On the third day, I was shown that the little boy had not magically brought the plague to his village, but had predicted that the deaths of most of the villagers would be caused by something in the water. The boy had told them not to drink the water, but they wouldn't listen. Instead they ridiculed him, poked and hit him with sticks, and said that he had gone mad. Those who survived blamed him for the deaths, and because witches and warlocks in those times were deemed evil, the boy was burned alive.

So how did this relate to me? During meditation about a week later, I saw the boy's face. His face was my face, even though I knew that my face was not the face he had in that life. I had seen a past life of mine.

Whether the vision and the sensations were real or not, they brought to the surface my fear of persecution for having the gifts I do. The experience encouraged me to analyse these gifts to understand why I feared using them. In the earlier chapter "Journey into the Unknown," I recounted how at a young age I was called a "freak" and "odd" because of these gifts, and in my undeveloped mind, I was persecuted for them.

When I realised I had lived and died in a previous life for using these gifts, something in me seemed to click into place. I emotionally and psychologically investigated my fear of persecution and came to understand that in this lifetime I would not be put to death or physically tormented. I saw that it was safe for me to continue my development and encourage these parts of myself to rise to the surface of my psyche. In doing so, I released a blockage in my heart, accepted that I would not suffer anymore, and began exploring my abilities.

What Is Reincarnation?

Reincarnation means that the soul, after physical death, begins a new life in a new body. Hinduism claims that the soul begins and ends in God because it is of God. Consequently the soul chooses to incarnate for learning, growth, and enlightenment.

When a soul enters the reincarnation cycle, it will incarnate many times to discover its true self and learn the lessons it needs. These involve understanding the God essence that lies within, and the process must be completed before the soul can merge fully and become one with the Creator.

What Is the Point of Reincarnation?

The point of reincarnation is to speed up our growth and enlightenment so that we recognise who and what we truly are. This is the realisation of the divine essence that lies within us, and we must accept in humility complete awareness of our own divinity before the soul can merge fully with the Creator. This is done by experiencing every facet of life, good or bad.

Reincarnation is about eventual fusion with the Creator and finding infinite peace and the state of being that this union offers. Reincarnation teaches us what we need to know by providing learning experiences in each life. Instead of behaving like primitive man, we evolve, become enlightened, and accept our spirituality. A soul in the early stages of the reincarnation cycle will kill or behave in sadistic and cruel ways even, when not mortally threatened. These souls operate according to self-serving impulses and display almost no self-control as they seek to fulfil their desires. Hence they are called baby or infant souls. Academic education doesn't matter in their development, since intelligence within the spirit realm is predominantly made up of sound and light frequencies, communicated through emotions, and what we learn academically is passed on as data via energetic vibrations. These souls may have many thousands of lives to live before they can behave like enlightened beings and pay off their karmic debts.

Past Lives and Karma

Buddhist teachings on the law of karma say that "for every event that occurs, there will follow another event whose existence was caused by the first, and this second event will be pleasant or unpleasant according to its cause being skilful or unskillful."[21]

A "skillful" event is unaccompanied by craving, resistance, or delusions, and an "unskillful" event is accompanied by any one of those things. The law of karma teaches that the person committing unskillful actions carries responsibility for them.

In the chapter "Differences between Mediums and Psychics," I mention the adages "What goes around comes around" and "What goes around comes around, and comes around tenfold." These are appropriate in describing karma. "As you sow, so shall you reap" is another fitting proverb that springs to mind. It also tells us that whatever we do will come back to us at some point. We must always be mindful of our behaviour and its consequences. For example, if an individual

---

[21] Dharma.ncf.ca. 1997. "The Law of Karma". Last modified October 1997. http://dharma.ncf.ca/introduction/truths/karma2.html.

has lived a lifetime as a racist, that person is likely to be a victim in a subsequent life, reincarnating as a member of a persecuted group.

While karma may contribute to the circumstances we face, each of us has free will to choose our reaction to an event. We can act out of love, compassion, and positivity, or out of fear, anger, and negativity. If we choose the latter, we will have opportunities to learn again in another life.

Can Past Life Regression Help?

Not all problems or issues originate from experiences in previous lifetimes, and it is important to determine if an issue must be addressed through other forms of therapy. Here are some reasons for using past life regression.

- Problematic behaviour and negative attitudes that have persisted over time despite attempts to alter these patterns.
- Unexplained relationship intensity, such as intense attraction or aversion to another person.
- Chronic fears, such as fear of spiders or fear of heights, that seem unconnected to the current life.
- Some long-standing physical ailments.
- Dealing with controlling emotions or attitudes that appear to continue throughout your life.
- Discovering strengths and accomplishments from previous lifetimes that can be used to increase confidence and success in this life cycle.
- Experiencing a happy former lifetime to gain clear thinking and strength when facing challenges in this life.
- Defining your direction and life purpose by viewing the soul's plan for this lifetime.
- Exploring previous lifetimes shared with current loved ones to learn why you are together in this life.

- Accessing wisdom, guidance, and love from the spiritual realm so that your higher self and your guides can evaluate your progress and give you direction.
- Raising awareness of the spiritual nature of existence.

Methods of Past Life Regression

Different methods can be used to access past lives. These methods typically include meditation, hypnosis, and self-hypnosis.

I use meditation, which works well for me. The downside of "do it yourself" past life recall occurs whilst watching what appears to be a television screen showing a program about your previous life. As you observe the scene, you may find that questions you wanted to ask are forgotten in your fascination with what you are seeing and feeling.

—ooOoo—

I am not offering instructions on how to recall a past life, since this is a very intimate journey and must be undertaken in the way best suited to each individual. I do not recommend doing it the way I did as a beginner, since I experienced emotional and mental exhaustion.

Although I continue to assist many people in past life recall, I do this through guided meditation techniques. These I have learnt the hard way! I wouldn't want anyone to walk the path I did in the quest for self-knowledge.

I have come to realise that this was one of my lessons in this lifetime. I was thrown into the deep end to guide others in what not to do!

As a result of my steep learning curve, I am now quite proficient in aiding others in recalling their past lives and would highly recommend the gentle guidance of a hypnotherapist or spiritual development teacher in the initial stages of past life recall. Let these skilled people assist you in your journey of self-discovery. It's a far kinder thing to do for yourself.

CHANNELLING

I spontaneously channelled for the first time at the age of twenty-seven. I had driven to Surrey in the UK to pick up a girlfriend so she could stay with me in London for the weekend. We lit candles and set about making our dinner, laughing and chatting the entire time. We ate our feast with relish. After our meal, we moved to more comfortable seating, my friend on a sofa and I in an armchair. We each had a glass of wine and were thoroughly enjoying the evening, talking and catching up on the other's news. Suddenly, I felt my body slump and become extremely heavy. I was unable to move, and my head felt like a vise had been clamped around it. My brain started pulsating and I began speaking. After about five minutes, I was released, my brain and head felt lighter, and I regained control of my body.

I was fully aware of everything that was taking place. Something within me seemed to move out of the way to make room for something else. I could hear myself speak, only I wasn't doing the talking. I heard via vibrations the noise coming out of my mouth. I couldn't fully hear the words as we do with our ears, and I sensed them as a movement of energy to my voice box to be released from my mouth. I felt no fear, particularly since the occurrence had been completely unexpected and I had no time to raise any protective barriers in response.

When I regained control of my body and my mind, I looked at my girlfriend whose face was the picture of shock. I asked her what had just happened (even though I knew without understanding). She told me that just before I spoke, she had seen my body slump, my face change to that of a wrinkled old woman, and my hands become gnarled and aged. My voice sounded older, and the words I spoke were not the kind I would normally use.

My friend told me she was shocked and afraid, since she had never seen anything like this before, so she didn't pay much attention to what was being said and couldn't completely recall all she had heard. She said that she recognised the lady, but wasn't sure where from, not initially anyway. She said that even though she was overcome by fear, she knew in her heart that she was safe and eventually realised that her late grandmother was speaking to her through me, using the words she used when she was alive, including the vernacular of her time. Now I understand that this was my first foray into trance channelling.

What is Channelling?

Channelling is a human being's communication with any consciousness that is not in human form. This is done by allowing an entity or a group of entities to speak through the channeller, using a number of methods, such as conscious and semiconscious/inspirational channelling.

Channelling usually requires a more evolved consciousness. It can assist in our spiritual growth and expand our awareness of life and the act of living.

When I am about to channel, my crown chakra generally receives indicators that an entity has approached me and wishes to communicate. I feel a compression, like a clamp being placed around my head. This is followed by a tingling in the crown area, and I feel a tickle in my throat. My neck then thickens as the entity adapts my voice box. Although this is the way channelling begins for me, your indicators may differ from mine. I have noticed that in both trance and deep trance channelling, channellers will say, "It feels like someone's playing with my throat."

It's unfortunate that movies habitually portray humans with extraordinary gifts and communication with the spirit world in a negative light. This along with gross exaggeration has created fear of the unknown. In the 1973 movie *The Exorcist*, a young girl is possessed by a demon; in the 1976 film *Carrie*, a girl abuses the gift of telekinesis after being bullied; and in the 1984 movie *Nightmare on Elm Street*, Freddie Kruger kills people in their sleep. These are all dreadfully negative depictions of spirit entities and our gifts.

I saw *Carrie* and *Nightmare on Elm Street* when I was a young girl. (No, my parents didn't let me see these films. I went to a friend's house to watch them.) I didn't sleep for months. My ten-year-old son was shown a picture of Freddie Kruger at school. The child who showed him the picture told my son that Freddie "gets you when you're asleep." We had ten weeks of no sleep, and no amount of reassurance worked.

Channelling an evolved entity or a group of entities is an experience founded in love, not fear. Done with pure intention and for the greater good of all involved, it can be a spiritually fulfilling experience that leaves you feeling enlightened, loved, and at peace.

Why Would Entities Want to Speak Through a Channel?

Channelled entities can be spirit guides, angels, or groups of entities, such as the sentinels from the Andromeda galaxy, whom I have channelled. Generally, those communicating are celestial teachers, such as Quan Yin, who reside in the land of spirit[22] with all other entities. Their vibrations are much finer than those of less learned souls who are still in the early stages of their growth. Generally, a channel will tune in to entities that have some significant connection to them, mainly through their religions or former religions. For example, a Christian is

---

[22] There are many schools of thought regarding the different planes where spirits reside. It is my belief that within the land of spirit, no being is separated by growth and learning into higher or lower planes of existence. It is my truth that we reside together with our soul families and are not restricted in our connections with other groups (unless we choose to be solitary for a while). However, our level of enlightenment, learning, and growth (before, during, and after an incarnation wherever that incarnation has taken place) is shown through the colour our soul/spirit radiates when we return to our original form and after any energy balancing work carried out on us.

likely to channel Jesus or Mary, and a Hindu will connect with Krishna. It is rare to see a person channel an entity from another religion.

I have found that beings wish to speak through a channel to deliver valuable messages to an individual or to group of people. They tend to do this when they attempt to communicate in other ways and are not heard. This is usually because the physical density of our body and our mind prevents an entity from being sensed. When we are not receptive, these entities or groups of beings will find a more direct way to communicate with us. Mediumship work is one form of channelling. The medium is fully conscious and receives the information, interprets it, then passes it on to the recipient. This is relay channelling.

What Are the Types of Channelling?

There are (as far as I'm aware) three types of channelling, which allow communications to be received from above.

1. **Conscious/relay channelling** allows the channel to hear or to see messages and to relay them to persons or to a group. These channels are fully conscious and aware of their surroundings.

2. **Semiconscious/inspirational channelling** involves a mixture of direct communication by the entity and the use of the channel's personality through which the information is interpreted. The channel's voice and mannerisms typically appear unchanged, although messages given can be profound.

   Automatic writing falls under this category. This occurs when a person begins writing without thinking about the content. Spirit entities communicating via this means usually deliver incredibly reflective insights for us to ponder.

   This is one of my favourite ways of writing, and even though I try not to let my views enter the communication, I'm aware that some may slip in. However, more often than not, once I have finished and review what has been written, I am struck by the straightforward way in which it has been conveyed.

Admittedly, as an ex-executive assistant (with a typing speed of about seventy to eighty words per minute), I have the advantage of typing quickly enough to keep up with an entity, whereas my handwriting is slow and cursive (in short, it looks pretty!). So using a computer to enable these entities to speak through me works exceptionally well.

I have conducted experiments with conscious and semiconscious/inspirational channelling in which I have chosen a topic, such as the meaning of wisdom, to discuss with friends. Frequently, my friends struggled to understand what I was trying to say. Interestingly, when I then allowed myself to be receptive to an evolved consciousness that stepped forward to channel, and we began speaking about the same topic, my friends told me that the information was not at all baffling and that they understood what was being said.

3. **Trance/deep trance channelling** allows the channel to completely relinquish his or her body so that the entity can converse through it. The soul moves out of the way to enable the entity to take over the body, and the being is allowed full and direct control over all speech and physical movement. The voice and physical mannerisms used by the spirit entity to communicate through the channel are usually dissimilar from the channel's.

An entity that has entered a human body to pass on its message can be limited in its communication by the vocabulary, bias, understanding, or learning of the human host. The reason for this is that the entity uses the channel's vocabulary database and life's experiences to convey the message. You may rightly wonder why a channelled entity would need to use the human's database when it is using the human's body to host its own essence.

From what I understand, this is because communication in the land of spirit is done through the simultaneous use of emotions, symbols, and vibrations, and this language has never been audible on earth. The channelling entity needs to translate its language upon entering a human's body. After merging with the human, the entity must use the channel's vocabulary and emotional and intellectual understanding so that humans can receive the communication in a familiar way.

However, the main aspect of the human that entities wish to use is the vocabulary database. That's because they want to speak and be clearly understood. Although the human's soul has made room for the channelled entity, the primal side of the human remains, and if this aspect feels that what is being conveyed is nonsense, it may well demand that the soul move back into place. The communicating entity will then be ejected from the host body. The human body and its soul interact through vibrations and emotions, and the soul will respond immediately to keep the human body as stress-free as possible.

I have heard of people deep trance channelling a highly evolved being, who when asked a challenging question, cannot respond because the human's mind intrudes and instills fear of being wrong. I believe that these beings can answer almost any question that we may pose, and would not flounder in their responses. However, it is not uncommon for an entity to refuse to answer a question if it feels the query is off topic or does not concern the enquirer's spiritual growth.

I can see an entity entering a channel's body through the base of the neck at the back of the head and can see auras fairly clearly with my eyes open. I see the channel's aura change to a brilliant gold colour, indicating that the merging is complete. If I do not see the entity enter the person and the aura change to gold, I know that the merging has not taken place, and that the individual is not in deep trance. When this happens and the channel relays a message, the person's biological mind may prevent full cooperation with the communicating entity, and the person's views will likely be added to the message.

Many deep trance channellers say they are unable to recollect what has been said. My experience of channelling differs. Though my soul (in its true energy form) makes way for an entity, it is still within my body, and although I am unable to see clearly (even if my eyes are open, my vision becomes blurred), I can hear and feel everything that is happening. (My spirit responds to the universal language of spirit.) Also, before my spirit completely moves aside, my body is unable to move, much like during deep hypnosis. This shows that people experience things in many ways.

I asked my spirit guide why I couldn't move my body when deep trance channelling. He responded that it is not necessary for entities to move the body to get their message across, since only our voice box is needed. He said that the only time they are likely to move the body is when they wish to touch a person, using the human's hands. However, to do this requires an enormous amount of their energy, which they try not to expend, since they have lowered their vibrations considerably to match the human vibration, encouraging ours to rise. He said that when entities use our bodies to communicate, they pass on healing to us in order not to exhaust us when our vibrations are raised to meet theirs. This is their gift to us for our assistance. They need a cleansing shower after each channelling to replenish and rebalance their energy after it has been housed in the channel's body even for a short while.

When we deep trance channel, physical ailments often leave our bodies because of the healing we have received.

People will often channel beings they are vibrationally able to handle. If an entity raises our vibration too high and we are not ready for it, stress can be created in the body. Entities that work with us (doorkeepers/gatekeepers, guardian angels, and guardian spirits) are acutely aware of this fact and will not allow a being to use our body as a vessel if this causes us distress. Simply put, we can channel only those entities with which we are vibrationally compatible and no more—until we raise our own vibrations.

What Do the Entities Say?

Unless an entity has specific information it wishes to impart and this is its sole reason for communication,[23] the questions of a person or group of people interacting with the entity usually determine the direction of the conversation. Therefore it is difficult to generalise about what entities say.

As individually unique as spirit entities are, they all seem to agree on certain fundamental universal truths that apply throughout all dimensions and realities. The fact that they agree, despite communicating through numerous unconnected channels at different times and in different eras and places, lends credibility to what they report involving existence outside the earth plane on all levels. Some of the things that they appear to agree on are:

* Everything is consciousness,[24] and everything, both animate and inanimate, has consciousness. In other words, nothing exists outside of consciousness. This consciousness perpetually pulsates with energy.

  In the chapter "Auras," I wrote, "Quantum physicists have confirmed what mystics and ancient civilizations have always known: that everything in the universe vibrates with energy. These scientists have accepted that we are more than just our physical bodies and that everything, including human beings and our thoughts and consciousness, is perpetually pulsating with energy at varying densities." These physicists are today discussing the many dimensions of existence that the ancients knew about. Where did these civilizations get their information about crystal healing or aura energy healing? Virtually all of them practiced these techniques. They didn't have telephones, and most of them wouldn't have known about cultures beyond their own. The only reasonable

---

[23] I understand this to mean that the entity will enter the channel, deliver its message, discourage questions, and disappear as quickly as it came.

[24] As I understand it, the word *consciousness* in this instance means intelligent awareness.

assumption is that they acquired their knowledge from a more evolved consciousness and trusted what they received.

I find it interesting that people thousands of years ago were so much more spiritually aware than we are today. We assert our superiority over ancient societies, claiming to be more advanced, and technologically and scientifically this is true. However, human beings have largely abandoned using the creative right-brain aspect of the self, embracing a scientific culture that uses the logical, analytical left brain. This change has prevented us from accepting what we see and feel beyond the physical, creating doubt and cynicism.

- Reincarnation exists, and earth is one of many realms in which a soul can incarnate to learn valuable lessons such as tolerance, kindness, acceptance, love, compassion, giving, receiving, and gentleness, to name a few. Refer to the chapter "Reincarnation and Past Lives."

- There is a universal law concerning the consequences of our actions, which are called karma. Refer to the chapter "Reincarnation and Past Lives" under the subtitle "Past Lives and Karma."

- Linear time does not exist. This is a man-made concept. The spirit entities say that time is nonexistent in the universe and that there is only the "now."

- We have the ability to create our individual reality. The spirit entities say that people design the conditions of their lives by thinking, feeling, and behaving as they do. The entities stress that "like attracts like." Like thoughts attract like thoughts, like actions attract like actions, in turn attracting other, more powerful like thoughts and like actions. When an individual perceives a thought or an action as positive or negative, this perception tends to intensify the person's response to the thought or the action. A positive thought or action will attract further positivity, just as a negative thought or action will attract negativity.

- There is no death as we know it. Once the body expires, the soul leaves the human form, which is seen by the soul as its clothes. The body is set aside, since it has served its purpose . . . until the next incarnation when it dons its new outfit.

Some of My Own Channellings

I have reproduced below a few messages received through my own inspirational channelling. The information sent does not reflect my normal thoughts, although I now spend a lot of time communicating with my higher mind (linked to the one consciousness), and most of my thoughts now seem to come from a greater reality. I have a much deeper understanding of universal energies and the alternate reality that lies beyond the earth realm.

Freedom

Given by the entity known as
Archangel Zadkiel on 16 April 2010

I, Archangel Zadkiel, come forth to speak of freedom.

The question often asked is "How do I obtain true freedom?" Humanity tends to think of freedom as release from oppression, allowing one to have freedom of thought, freedom of speech, freedom of religious studies, and freedom of political views. Those living in countries considered first-world nations often confuse freedom with physical or financial liberty: the ability to go where you wish and spend what you like.

All these things are, of course, desirable, and the rights of human beings have been affirmed historically, though at great cost. Those who have not achieved these freedoms, whether through their own fault or by the hand of others, are often pitied and thought of as unfortunate.

So the question that one perhaps should ask is, "What is true freedom?" and not "How do I obtain true freedom?" Understanding the former will give you the answer to the latter.

Every person on this planet can find the true meaning of the words *freedom* or *liberation* simply by looking within. When one attains liberation in the inner world, one can find ways towards freedom in the outer world. People are bound by their own fears, which keep them climbing the steep mountain, only to glimpse its peak, then slide down to the bottom to start over again. Self-doubt, fear of the unknown, fear of failure, fear of being disliked, fear of not being good enough, or perhaps the inability to believe in their own sanity—the list is endless.

However, amid all the bleakness comes a golden ray of light that will show each human being a unique path to ultimate liberation. All one need do is truly want it. The heart and the soul know if the intention is genuine.

The shadow self, or what you call the ego, is a fierce master! Or is it? The shadow self, believe it or not, was actually a somewhat immature ally in the world as it was. The world is now moving to a new age of enlightenment. How?

In the world as it was, the fears that the shadow self harboured helped your species to survive. Much like in the current animal kingdom, instincts were heavily relied upon. Fears kept you alert and alive.

When you turn into yourself and truly see yourself, you are often afraid. Our advice is, do not fear that which you can control, for the fact is that you can control your shadow self if you so choose. Although this may take some effort, your ability is testament to the divine being that you are. For you were formed from the love of the divine. Whatever name you call your God, this is one in the same entity.

Embrace your shadow self and invite it to merge with your divine self, and in this merging you will find your true self, your only self, and the balance of self to be your higher self. Have faith in yourself, and your light will burst forth brighter than any star you see in the night sky.

If you seek, you will find the way. All you need do is ask with intention, and it shall be done.

To you, our brothers and sisters, we send our blessings and deepest love. Walk in the path of truth, freedom, and love, and you shall always be in the light, for we are all one.

Acceptance

*Given by the entity known as Torquits, teacher
of truth guide, on 3 August 2010*

The life of man is riddled with doctrines that are passed down throughout the ages. These forms of indoctrination create the belief systems that are in place today.

Very few people begin their lives on the path of true spirituality. They spend their formative years searching for the meaning of life and death. This search will lead them to many religions and to people who they hope will reveal the mystery.

The majority have, during their most tender years, been influenced by beliefs and opinions of others, so when they do eventually find their own unique spiritual path, they cannot embark on it with an unbiased heart and mind and fully comprehend what spiritual enlightenment is about. Their new experiences contradict what they have been taught, and this leads to confusion and frustration.

Our advice to you who are seekers is to try to relinquish all your previous belief systems so that you are a blank canvas. Please be gentle with yourselves when doing this, for it can take time and the release of old tenets can create fear. Do not be afraid to seek the assistance of those in a position to help you.

When you have released old indoctrinated principles, the alteration in your mind and body will be evident. You will have a sense of unrestricted freedom, which can be felt in your brow, heart, and solar plexus chakras. When this has been achieved, your soul, unencumbered by burdens, will invite the new learning that your higher self and spirit bring. Your personal truth is very different from another's, for each person and his or her path are unique.

What is revealed to another may never be revealed to you and vice versa, for your revelations are meant only for you. This does not mean that your experiences are better than another's or that another's are better than yours. Keeping an open, accepting heart and mind, even when you have not had another person's experience, will allow you to keep absorbing information for your betterment and the betterment of mankind. By keeping the portal open, you can guide others on their unique paths without influencing or being influenced. This is called acceptance.

Acceptance that all have a right to believe as they will. Acceptance that yours is not the only way. When this acceptance takes place, human beings will begin to feel unity with one another. Religious warfare will cease. Bigotry will be laid to rest, and the desire to control through fear will no longer be. Acceptance will bring a fairer economic climate no longer based on materialism, and global leaders will become more genuinely concerned with the state of world affairs.

Fear and Control

Given by the entity known as
Archangel Zadkiel on 19 January 2011

The doubt that some hold within their hearts as to the existence of spirit entities and structures not visible to the human eye is a direct result of deeply ingrained fear over the loss of control. Humans used to see until fear and the desire for control were introduced by those who wished to be worshipped as gods aeons ago. This fear and desire for control remain, as humans continue to instil terror in a bid to gain power.

Human intellect has always believed that "what we control we therefore own." This is clear from the behaviour patterns of the species. Humans think that they create order out of chaos with this basic instinct. It is not so. This type of control creates disharmony, because those seeking power oppress the masses. This negative energy has a vibrational ripple effect across entire continents, and this is passed to the universal grid that shifts all matter. Earth is not the only planet affected by this human diffusion of cynicism. The entire universe suffers because of the deeds of despots.

Yet there is much to rejoice in, because mankind is beginning to awaken and recognise this trait based on egotistic attitudes. Never before have so many been able to comprehend what is at stake, yet there is still much to do.

When people face the arduous task of bringing into alignment their egocentric tendencies with what they know deep within themselves by uniting the polarities of the conscious mind with the higher mind, the questions raised, along with the task at hand, can be daunting. Do not allow yourself to see the assignment in a negative light. Intent and desire are progressive, and both states are comparatively easy to attain.

Do not be shackled by your own sense of worth as dictated by others who do not feel worthy. Freedom is within you and is yours for the taking if you desire.

In light, love, peace, joy, and harmony, children of the earth, we honour your divine beauty. Bring yourselves into balance, and to you shall come that which you seek.

Message of Growth

Given by my higher self on 25 January 2011

When people approach their life paths with open hearts, they allow themselves to embark on the amazing journey of self-discovery.

When the heart is receptive, the mind can accept the inner growth that will inevitably happen. This can involve confrontation, since old belief systems are being challenged. When these obstacles are faced and overcome, the personal journey can continue unburdened by the influence of others. The challenge is then to prevent the conscious mind from curtailing personal advancement. This is not easy and requires fortitude and perseverance, since most people have lived under the control of the conscious mind all their lives. There are also the doctrines of the subconscious and unconscious minds to contend with. These are deeply embedded emotions that the conscious mind has decided the body, due to its experience, is unable to handle.

These elements of human spirit are not what the person is. But they are a part of what humans need to survive. They can, with desire and intent, be altered and rewired for your betterment.

Growth is not to be feared. It should be welcomed because it brings self-awareness and, ultimately, inner peace. Honour your metamorphosis, and seek your inner truth, for the universe lies within. From there, your higher self can answer all your questions without reservation.

Cosmic Consciousness

*Given by a group consciousness I know as the sentinels
from the Andromeda galaxy on 29 January 2011*

The cosmic consciousness is so vast that it is outside the reach of human comprehension at this stage of evolution, no matter how advanced humans think they may be. There is an ordered structure in which are recorded all celestial deeds and events that have occurred and that are still occurring throughout time and space, including those on your planet. These records enable teachers to reveal fragments to inhabitants of the earth for their education when they commence their growth cycles.

These records are not intended to limit the progress of mankind. Until enough of the inhabitants awaken their souls from their slumber,[25] this is simply esoteric information that cannot be assimilated into the consciousness of the species as a whole.

Here communication is achieved via emotions and symbols sent through vibrations. These vibrations are then converted instantaneously into words and feelings quite unlike your human ones. Our words and feelings are both audible and telepathic, depending on what is needed during the interaction. It is difficult to convey, but the best way to explain is that we converse using all senses simultaneously.

If human beings were able to access all the knowledge available, they would revert to the primal instinct of survival, which is based upon fear. Many already wrestle with the legitimacy of what has, over aeons,

---

[25]   When this was given to me, I didn't take the word *slumber* to mean sleeping. I felt it meant the limitations of the human mind. That's my interpretation. By all means interpret the word according to your understanding.

been revealed in many ways concerning the existence of the source and the alternate dimensions that surround you. There are still too many humans who would deny themselves awareness by blinkered views, thus closing themselves off to what we know would give the joy and contentment that all desire. Proof has always been visible. Open your heart, eyes, and higher mind to it.

In our observations of your species, we have gained an understanding of your limitless divinity when in your original form. Yet, bound by the solid configuration of the human frame and restricted by the power of fear, you are prevented from believing in your divinity. Until you have a true belief in who you are, we are unable to unlock the door to the entire universal intelligence, since we do not wish to cause you further doubt in your philosophies.

We do believe, however, that in time, as humans learn to blend the separate qualities of self and to trust that they are more than just a physical body and human mind, they will bring together the arts of science and theology, thereby granting themselves permission to fully explore and find answers to that which they have always sought.

Psychic Attack and Protection

Afew years ago whilst updating my résumé on my home computer, I doubled over in pain. It felt like someone had punched me in the stomach, and suddenly I felt incredibly nauseous. I ran to the bathroom, thinking I was going to be sick.

I yelled out to my husband, who asked me if I had eaten anything that might make me feel that way. He posed a lot of other questions in an attempt to narrow down what was making me feel so weak and queasy. We could not work out the cause no matter how we tried. After a few days of being unable to move and feeling like my life was draining away, I told my husband, "I don't want to die. I'm going to have to see the doctor. I swear something's trying to kill me!" Stroking my hair as I rested my head on his lap, Nick said, "Honey, you <u>are not</u> going to die. Not on my watch anyway!" God bless him. Those were the most soothing words he could have uttered in my time of need. After a while, I lay on my bed and meditated, hoping that would make me feel better.

In the act of silence, a sentence flashed before my inner eye. "Beware. You have been psychically attacked, and—is doing it daily." At that point, I had no idea of what a psychic attack was.

I had been given the name of the perpetrator, and the writing appeared to be cursive (much like my own), well-defined, and brilliant white. I had absolutely no idea what it meant, so I dragged myself to the computer to do some research.

All the symptoms I read about appeared to match mine, and because I am normally healthy and have an abundance of energy, the way I was feeling was very uncharacteristic. I was constantly tired, queasy, weak, and paranoid about my survival, and dread would wash over me at the thought of seeing a particular person with whom I had quarrelled. Furthermore, this individual also had an interest in magic, though at the time I did not take this seriously.

However, after identifying who was attacking me, I was able to defuse the attack with the help of Archangel Michael, strengthen my energy bodies, and create appropriate defences around me. Within hours of my aura being cleansed and protected, my health improved considerably. I was no longer exhausted, nauseous, or weak. I stopped feeling like my time was running out.

I did not send the negative energy back to the originator, since I felt this would be counterproductive and was unsure if it would add to my karma. Now I realise that would not have been the case, particularly if my intent was not to harm but to educate.

Interestingly, once we resolved our issues, I told this person, "I swear you psychically attacked me!" The person responded, "I probably did!" This indicated knowledge and understanding of what psychic attacks are. I know that this individual would have denied doing it if this had been the case. If you are aware of what psychically attacking another person involves, there is no "probably" about it. Either you did or did not intentionally attack another person. Whoever or whatever produced that sentence in my mind's eye was correct. The attack was done with the intention of doing harm, and for a while it had been successful.

As a result of that psychic attack, I now clear, balance, and protect my energy field every day.

The words we direct at others are made up of vibrations. Mix those words with mental images of what you would like to happen to a person, and the energy becomes exceptionally potent. The words and images hit the intended target with unerring accuracy, and when they do, the effects can be traumatic, as they were for me.

What the attacker does not always realise is that conscious assaults usually incur karma for the sender in this lifespan or another life cycle and this karma will have to be settled. In many cases, the debt will be paid in the current lifetime.

What Is Psychic Attack?

A psychic attack generally involves the manipulation and movement of negative energies. These damaging energies are transferred into another person's energetic bodies, commonly known as the aura. They then can attack the physical body, creating emotional, psychological, and health issues, sometimes simultaneously. A psychic attack is generally carried out by another person or a group of people.

When a psychic attack occurs, you will usually feel exposed and vulnerable, and occasionally, depending on the strength of the onslaught, a sense of foreboding, personal danger, anxiety, or panic may ensue. In my case, my health and state of mind rapidly declined.

However, the negative energies that enter our homes or auras are generally unconsciously sent. Unconscious psychic attacks often happen among family members who interact dysfunctionally. But even if they are aware that their behaviour is damaging, they most likely don't realise that they are psychically assaulting each other.

Unconscious psychic attacks often occur in our places of work where people may not connect with colleagues or managers. When the job is linked to life-and-death situations or to circumstances that may involve confrontations, the chances of psychic attack rise considerably. Police officers, firefighters, members of the armed forces, lawyers, doctors, nurses, and paramedics, for instance, would be at particular risk. In these cases, the attack is generally directed against the uniform or the authority it represents rather than the people themselves. Unfortunately, negative energy does not differentiate between a uniform and a person, and the individual suffers the full brunt of the assault.

An unconscious psychic attack could also happen when a person does not like you, and you may not even be aware of how this person feels.

Conversely, there are those who purposefully send negative energies with the intention of seeking revenge, causing harm, manipulating or controlling another person. These attacks can involve ceremonial practices, psychic powers, or a combination of both. More often than not, with the untrained,[26] it is the intense dislike or hatred that they project to their target that forms the attacking energy. These psychic attackers do not usually know what they are doing. They simply want the other person to suffer.

There are a myriad of reasons for psychic attacks, and it is impossible to list them all. However, you can detach yourself emotionally from a situation, a person, or a group if you can accept that not everyone will like or agree with you. In doing so, you will stop giving your energy to others who have no appreciation for it. If you adopt a level of acceptance, psychic attacks will have less impact on your aura, and you will not feel so drained.

It is difficult for a strong and healthy aura to be penetrated. Energy bodies are weakened by the regular use of drugs, alcohol, and cigarettes, and by emotional repression. Negative feelings about life also harm the aura. Physical ailments and/or disease can also severely damage the human energy field, and it is worth noting that most physical disorders start in the outer layers of our energy bodies, eventually moving through these levels to embed themselves in the physical body. Therefore maintenance and protection of your aura are essential to preventing psychic attacks from having a negative effect on your physical, emotional, and psychological well-being.

Warning Signs of Psychic Attack

There are many symptoms that suggest an attack by negative energies. Here is a list identifying a few of the main indicators. These

---

[26] The untrained, in this case, are those people who have not enhanced their psychic abilities. They generally do not know how to tap into another person's energy, and intentionally send the energy of hatred towards their victim. This is done by constantly having an inner dialogue with themselves, which consists of their hatred or dislike of the other person or group of people. Eventually, this inner dialogue of thought forms manifests, and make their way to the recipient, who then undergoes an attack on their aura.

signs can also point to common health problems, and it is important to investigate all possibilities.

- A sudden feeling that you have been punched in the stomach when nobody is near.
- Unexpected fatigue, weakness, or nausea, particularly if you are normally healthy. If you are a woman who suspects you may be pregnant, these symptoms are obviously not indicators of psychic attack.

  Be aware that fatigue and/or a sense of weakness often occur at certain times of the day. Generally, most of us will hit the wall between 2 and 4 p.m. each day. This is known as the postprandial dip,[27] a metabolism phenomenon. This is not a psychic attack. If your daily fatigue inexplicably increases, a psychic attack may be occurring.
- Unexpected changes such as memory loss, muddled thinking, loss of confidence or analytical ability, depression without apparent cause, illogical fear, anger, or sorrow, discomfort and fear in a room where you had felt secure, and obsessive negative thought processes that were previously not there.
- An icy cold feeling in parts or all of your body.
- A rise in misfortune at odds with your normal circumstances.
- Visions and/or hallucinations that include a particular voice that you regularly hear when you are nowhere near the person, recurrent nightmares with the same theme, and monsters or dark shadows that you imagine are around you.
- Feeling that you are being watched by someone or something or that someone aggressively bumped into you when no one is present.

---

[27] Postprandial dip is a term for mild hypoglycemia (a state produced by a lower-than-normal level of blood glucose, or sugar) occurring after digestion of a heavy meal. The dip is thought to be caused by a drop in blood glucose resulting from the body's normal insulin secretion, a response to the glucose load represented by the meal. Postprandial dip can produce irresistible sleepiness in some individuals, leading to a postprandial nap.

- Sudden illnesses that medical professionals are unable to reasonably explain.
- Mysterious financial or relationship difficulties.
- Strange or recurring accidents.
- Feeling drained of energy whenever you are around a particular person or group of people.

Though this list is by no means comprehensive, it indicates what to look for when your life mysteriously changes.

Each person will have his or her own signs and symptoms when psychically attacked. If you are unsure whether negative energies are assaulting you, and you have sought appropriate medical and/or psychological advice and found no reasonable cause, consult an energy worker who has experience in identifying and clearing negative energies after attacks.

Clearing Your Aura and Protecting Yourself from Psychic Attack

Listed below are the methods I have used to expel negative energies and protect myself when psychically attacked.

Once you have cleared and protected your aura, it is important to periodically reinforce the protection. I always shield myself in the morning, but I generally seek new strength in the afternoon just before I hit the wall and become more vulnerable. I usually get an indication that I have received this strength when I feel a gentle squeezing sensation over my body (a bit like being given a bear hug, only not quite so uncomfortable). Your signs may be different, and you may not feel like you have been given a signal. Try not worry if this is the case, and believe it has been done. When I first started protecting myself, I felt nothing in response to my requests. It took months before I was receptive enough to recognise my indicators, and I had to trust that I was being protected.

There are many more ways to protect yourself than those listed here, but these are the ones I use, and they work well for me. I also recommend reading all you can on psychic defence and psychic vampirism.[28]

Most of my own research was done on the Internet; some of what I found worked, and some did not. I tried most of the suggestions for clearing my energy field and was only partially successful, though that does not mean that these suggestions would not work for you.

The spinning tornado of blue light is most effective for me, and this is not a strategy that I got from research. This technique came to me when I called on Archangel Michael for help.

The other methods listed have worked for me. I have adapted some to suit my needs. It is important to note that what succeeds for me might not work for you. Do not be afraid to experiment and change these strategies to meet your needs.

How to Expel Negative Energies from Your Aura and Protect Yourself

1. **Spinning Tornado of Blue Light:** This is an excellent method for expelling negative energies from your aura. I will provide a full description of my experience to offer a better understanding of the process.

   If you do not see or feel anything, simply know that the process is taking place. I had no expectations when this first occurred, and even though I always use the spinning tornado of blue light to clear my aura, I have not seen Archangel Michael again. I trust and know that my aura has been unblocked.

---

[28] Psychic vampirism is the work of a person or group of people who drain your energy. We have all at some point in our lives felt exhausted when we've been in the company of another person. We feel like the life has been drained out of us. This happens when another person consciously or unconsciously taps into your energy field and absorbs your energy so that he or she feels more vitalized. This is another form of psychic attack, and usually a good night's sleep or an aura clearing will replenish your energy levels.

It was a monumental moment in my life when I first requested help from Archangel Michael to remove harmful energies from my aura. Because of the old indoctrinated belief that archangels do not talk to mere mortals, I thought I was unworthy of his help. Had I not been feeling like death was coming for me, I would not have bothered him. But I plucked up my courage and asked, and I am extremely glad I did.

Imagine my surprise when he stood before me, sword in hand and brilliant white, iridescent wings outspread. His face was utterly beautiful, almost too exquisite to look upon, and he smiled at me. His hair was fair, but not quite blonde, and hung to his shoulders. This glorious being's eyes were electric blue, the same colour that radiated from him. The power he emanated was more potent than anything I had ever felt. No human words could do justice to this mighty being. With him was another angel who also emitted blue, though a little less electric a colour. Sadly, I was totally dazzled by Michael and did not pay close attention to the other angel, which I regret. I do recall that his wings were white, but the tips appeared to be a very pale grey.

Michael wrapped his wings around himself and began to spin, slowly at first. As he was spinning, his wings unfurled and he brandished his sword before him. His spinning accelerated, and he moved through and around my energy bodies with the sword. I remember thinking that he looked like a tornado. He used his sword to cut away the more destructive cords attached to me. The severed cords were created during my childhood, teenage, and adult years as well as by my psychic attacker. As they were being cut, I instinctively knew to whom each cord related. This process of cleansing continued for thirty minutes.

As Michael was clearing my energy field, the other angelic being spread his wings wide. As he did, I noticed all the negative energies severed from my aura being drawn into what appeared to be a strange six-sided box that he was holding in his arms.

When Michael finished clearing me, the container held by the other angel began to glow. I saw the colours of the rainbow through its translucent walls. Its contents seemed to be undergoing purification. I do not know what they did with the container once they left. However, Michael left me with these words: "Never fear your worth, for all are worthy. Child, your aura is cleared, and now you must place protection around you."

No matter how the spinning tornado of blue light comes to you, accept it. Sent with the purest of intentions, its effects are exceptional. They were for me, and I sincerely hope they are for you.

2. **Dome of White Light Protection:** Ask for a dome of white light to be placed around you. Imagine it as a bubble, and do not worry if you cannot feel it or see it in your mind's eye. The simple act of asking for help will ensure that you receive this protection.

3. **Gold or Silver Halo:** Once you have asked for a dome of white light to surround you, a gold or silver halo can be placed outside of the bubble. You may find that you want to use both colours. I usually use both when I have to visit Melbourne's central business district.

   Gold is associated with the divine masculine energy and silver with the divine feminine energy. These represent yang and yin (male/female) balance. Both colours are representative of divine protection.

   Once in a while, I may infuse these colours with pink, usually when I am advising someone. Pink is the colour associated with unconditional love.

4. **Electric Blue Cloak and Mask:** Because blue is the colour of Archangel Michael, who is known as the protector or warrior angel, this is an excellent colour for self-defence. Picture an electric-blue cloak being wrapped around your aura. Imagine yourself pulling the hood over your head and a mask falling into place. See yourself zipping up the cloak from under your feet to your chin. Know that you are completely protected.

5. **Mirrors:** You can also protect yourself by imagining mirrors surrounding you. Picture them placed above your head, below your feet, and to the front, back, and sides of your body. These mirrors face outward, reflecting all negative energies away from you.

6. **Four Spirit Warriors:** When I sense an attack by a person or a group of people, I ask the four spirit warriors for protection; they are enormous and remind me of Roman centurions.

   When lessons go unlearnt and cruel attacks are under way, I will ask the universe to send these warriors, who represent north, south, west, and east, to surround me. They provide defence by keeping their backs to me and their shields facing outward. Their spears rest upon their shoulders, angled skyward so the tips meet one another above my head.

   The spears are not symbolic of entering battle. They represent defence, and the spear tips signify protection of my crown chakra. These warriors project their light around me, returning all negative energies to the originator. They do not send back the energies to do harm but to teach. The destructive energies returned to the sender are not diluted. They have the same potency with which the attacker sent them. The objective is for the perpetrator of the psychic attack to understand the impact of what he or she is doing.

   These warriors will not aid in attacking a person, an animal, a place, or an object. They will not contribute to any abuse of power. They exist to protect, and their purpose is not destruction.

   I request the protection of these wise and powerful beings only in the case of emergencies when a psychic attack is prolonged and the attacker will not stop.

7. **Smudging with Sacred White Sage:** Native American Indians have used sacred white sage in their ceremonies for centuries. Refer to the chapter on auras under the subtitle "Strengthening and Refreshing the Aura" for instruction on smudging.

8. **Cord Cutting:** If you know your attacker, then a cord cutting exercise could be beneficial. You can sever the cord connecting

that person to you. There may be more than one cord, and you are most likely unaware of this. The best way of cutting cords is to meditate or sit quietly and call the person's higher self to you. Ask for Archangel Michael's assistance in cutting the cords.

Only one person's higher self has refused my request to come. When a person's higher self appears (or you sense this presence), explain that you wish to cut the cords that bind you so that both of you can get on with your lives. I realise this part may be difficult, particularly when the attack has been especially nasty or you have come from a dysfunctional family. However, if you tell the higher self that you wish the person no ill and that you release this person with love, this will discourage the attachment of other cords. Then ask Archangel Michael to cut the cords linking you.

Those with whom you cut the cord are likely to sense that you are no longer connected. They may consciously or unconsciously attempt to relink you to themselves, and unless you want this to happen, I suggest you regularly strengthen the defence of your aura so that reconnection cannot occur.

In the chapter on auras, I have described ways in which you can reinforce and replenish your aura. There you will find other useful methods for aura strengthening.

On a practical level, if you are unable to avoid a person or a group of people who you feel are detrimental to you, crystals can play a protective role. They can be placed in a pocket and kept with you all day and may be used in conjunction with any of the methods described above. Refer to the chapter on crystals to determine which stone may suit your needs.

EPILOGUE

During my journey, I have made huge personal changes, allowing me to benefit from previously unnoticed opportunities.

I have gained a deeper understanding of who I am, including my triggers and reactions to people and events, and the obstacles I have faced and overcome have encouraged acceptance in all aspects of my life. Through a greater self-awareness, I have been blessed with a more accepting, less critical view of life and the world in which I live.

I use the word *accepting* because it is now a significant part of my philosophy. Until I embarked on this journey, I did not realise that I lacked acceptance. I was judgemental, opinionated, jaded, angry, and lacked confidence in my talents.

Acceptance has let me open my heart and my mind to all possibilities around and within me. By accepting myself for who I am, including all those sides that I did not like, I have allowed my spirit to rise within me, bringing with it gifts I never knew I had.

I also have learned to accept others and their viewpoints, which makes for wonderful discussions. Variety is the spice of life, and each of us is unique, as are our personal journeys and experiences.

Another term might be applicable for you, perhaps self-belief or trust. If this is the case, consider how this term might change your perspective on life and the act of living. Words are powerful, and in finding the one that has meaning for me, I have given myself permission to start living my life and stop simply existing.

Everything you experience will be unique to you. No two people will have the same view of a scene they are observing together. Each will give different descriptions of that scene, and while those descriptions may be similar, there will at least be marginal differences.

If several people are seated in a room and all but one swaps chairs, the view presented of the person who has not moved will be different for all those who have switched places. For example, someone originally facing the individual who remained seated might then see this person's profile, which he may not previously have noticed.

This analogy shows that different views of the same situation can change the way in which we look at circumstances. These perceptions present opportunities for growth.

Believing in ourselves is vital, and with courage, determination, and the help of our spirit, we can watch our dreams come true.

You may find this surprising, but I never used to have dreams or aspirations. However, in discovering my dreams, I faced my fear of rejection and criticism, and pursued them. One of those dreams was to write this book, so I decided to try. The words seemed to flow. I have not been taught how to write, certainly not for publication, though I've always written poetry. However, I now have a passion for writing, and no matter what, I intend to keep doing it.

I realised that my fears could no longer hurt me and that my more disturbing memories were in place to keep me from perceived harm, but they were in fact doing more damage. This insight has enabled me to drive away the inner demons that held me hostage for so long, and in doing so, I am now able to achieve my dreams. The most rewarding part of all the hard work is the inner peace I have discovered.

Acceptance, self-belief, courage, determination, self-awareness, and my spirit have brought me unconditional self-love, and that is the greatest gift that I could have offered myself.

I have lost nothing and gained everything during this journey.

Enjoy your own journey, knowing that you can only grow stronger and brighter in your self-discoveries.